FOUNDER
H.E.R.O.

A HOLISTIC PATH TO PURPOSE DRIVEN SUCCESS

BY CHRIS COLL AND JAMES ARTMAN

Copyright © 2025

All rights are reserved, and no part of this publication may be reproduced, distributed, or transmitted in any manner, whether through photocopying, recording, or any other electronic or mechanical methods, without the explicit prior written permission of the publisher. This restriction applies to any form or means of reproduction or distribution.

Exceptions to this rule include brief quotations that may be incorporated into critical reviews, as well as certain other noncommercial uses that are allowed by copyright law. Any such usage must adhere to the specified conditions and permissions outlined by the copyright holder.

Book Design by HMDPublishing.com

CONTENTS

PREFACE 5
INTRODUCTION 15

CHAPTER 1
HOW TO USE THIS BOOK. 20

CHAPTER 2
INTRODUCTION TO FOUNDER MODE 34

CHAPTER 3
THE FOUNDER'S MINDSET.. 43

CHAPTER 4
FOUNDATIONAL HEALTH FOR FOUNDERS.. ... 71

CHAPTER 5
MASTERING EMOTIONAL AND SPIRITUAL INTELLIGENCE 81

CHAPTER 6
LIFE IS FULL OF CHOICES 101

CHAPTER 7
CURATING YOUR ENVIRONMENT FOR SUCCESS .... .106

CHAPTER 8
INTRODUCTION TO THE FOUR PILLARS. 119

CHAPTER 9
MENTAL RESILIENCE — FOUNDATIONAL THINKING
FOR PURPOSE-DRIVEN SUCCESS. 148

CHAPTER 10
PHYSICAL RESILIENCE. 161

CHAPTER 11
SPIRITUAL RESILIENCE 172

CHAPTER 12
ENVIRONMENTAL RESILIENCE........................184

CHAPTER 13
HARNESSING WEALTH RESILIENCE....................218

CHAPTER 14
FOUNDER FULLFILLMENT DRIVES BUSINESS SUCCESS....224

CHAPTER 15
THE MODERN-DAY FOUNDER'S BLUEPRINT............231

CHAPTER 16
SCALING WITH PURPOSE............................241

CHAPTER 17
SUSTAINING FOUNDER H.E.R.O......................247

ACKNOWLEDGMENTS..............................259

REFERENCES...................................264

PREFACE

I believe every human being encounters trials and tribulations early in life that profoundly influence the trajectory and direction their journey takes. These defining moments shape who we are and who we become, often testing the very fabric of our resilience. Each person responds to adversity in their own way. Some are consumed by it, while others find a way to transform pain into purpose. This book is a culmination of my journey—Chris Coll—along with the experiences of my co-founder and true friend, James Artman. Together, we have traversed paths of healing that ultimately converged, enabling us to create something meaningful to share with the world.

No one experiences trauma in exactly the same way, and no two traumatic events are identical. However, there exists a universal truth: anyone can learn a system to overcome tragedy, trauma, and adversity. Life will inevitably throw challenges our way, and when it does, this system serves as a lifeline, enabling us to choose resilience over despair. It equips us to step out of the victim mindset and take control of our lives. Make no mistake, this is not easy. Acknowledging the reality of being a victim is valid, but living with that mentality only perpetuates pain and suffering. To truly heal and grow, we must break free from that cycle and embrace the power within us to thrive.

My journey, like Jim's, has been shaped by deeply personal experiences that molded me into the person I am today. Early in my entrepreneurial path, I faced a significant and devastating loss—one that would forever alter my perspective on life. I lost my father suddenly and unexpectedly, right in front of me. The shock, the grief, and the trauma of that moment were overwhelming, but they also ignited a profound realization: life is short. My dad instilled a belief in me that guides me everyday "Everything happens for a reason." Instead of wallowing in how could this happen to me? How could my dad be gone? I approached his loss as a lesson & gave it more purpose than I could have possibly imagined at the time. Mindset is just one focus in our system of *Founder H.E.R.O: A Holistic Path to Purpose Driven Success*, but my dad's death served a significant purpose in my life. It was undoubtedly a tragedy, but it opened the door of the realization that we only get one chance, and every day matters. My dad served this country for 37 years between the Navy & DOD, he sacrificed his life to serve this country and wouldn't trade it for any other life. His purpose gave way for me & any US citizen to freely live in pursuit of his or her own purpose. From that moment forward, I vowed to lead my life with purpose and intention, refusing to let fear or doubt dictate my actions. This loss became a catalyst for growth, driving me to channel my pain into something greater—something that could inspire others to do the same.

Jim and I have vastly different stories. Our individual journeys are marked by unique traumas and challenges, yet we share a common understanding: trauma doesn't define you; how you respond to it does. For us, it wasn't about comparing whose pain was greater or whose experiences were more severe. Instead, we recognized our respective struggles as opportunities for transformation. Through self-discovery, perseverance, and an unyielding commitment to growth, we turned our pain into a foundation for resilience—a foundation that now underpins everything we do.

Three years ago, I met Jim on the set of Season 3 of the competitive, entrepreneurial TV show - *The Blox,* hosted by Wes Bergmann - the self proclaimed smartest & sexiest redhead in the world (his words) from MTV's hit show -*The Challenge*, a chance encounter that would change both our lives. From that initial week-long encounter, we forged a bond that has since grown into a friendship and partnership rooted in a shared mission.

Together, we founded Extreme Resilience and the non-profit Resilient Recovery NC, organizations dedicated to empowering others to overcome adversity and reclaim their lives. Our motto, "Own Your Purpose," reflects the essence of our journey and the principles we strive to impart.

This book is more than a collection of stories; it is a guide to embracing vulnerability and stepping into what we call 'Founder H.E.R.O.' By adopting this mindset, you can unlock your potential and become the best version of yourself in every area of life—health, wealth, business, and personal relationships. Through our unique insights and experiences, we hope to inspire you to lead with purpose, no matter what challenges you face.

Life is not without its struggles, but it is through those struggles that we find strength, meaning, and the ability to create something extraordinary. My hope is that this book will provide you with the tools and inspiration to navigate your own journey with resilience, courage, and purpose. So, here is Jim's story of resilience, followed by the lessons we've learned together. May it serve as a beacon of hope and a call to action for anyone ready to embrace their own power and potential.

James Artman's Story of Resilience: A Journey from War to Healing

SSG James Artman (spotter) on a blown up roof top in support of Operation Iraqi Freedom V.

Resilience is a concept often misunderstood as mere toughness or an unyielding ability to endure. In truth, it's much more nuanced, dynamic, and profoundly human. My journey from the battlefields as an Army Ranger and Sniper, to guiding others in building purpose-driven lives has taught me that resilience isn't a static trait but a skill-set forged in the fires of hardship, tempered by self-awareness, and honed through intentional healing.

The Call to Serve

Like many young men with a deep sense of duty, I joined the military to serve something greater than myself. The Army Rangers, (75th Ranger Regiment) are known for their rigorous selection process and high standards, which drew me to the challenge. Over time, I earned my place in this elite group and later took on the role of a sniper and later a sniper school instructor at Ft. Benning, GA—a position requiring intense focus, precision, and mental fortitude.

The years in service shaped me in countless ways. They sharpened my discipline, strengthened my resolve, and taught me the value of teamwork by always choosing not to quit, give up or try less. But they also exposed me to the relentless toll of high-stakes operations, physical exhaustion, and the emotional weight of combat. Like many veterans, I bore the scars of those experiences—not all of which were visible.

From Battlefield to Breaking Point

Transitioning from military life to the civilian world is a challenge few truly understand. The structure, camaraderie, and adrenaline that defined my identity were suddenly gone, leaving me adrift. In their place came isolation, frustration, and the haunting memories of my time in combat. Post-traumatic stress became a silent companion, one that quietly infiltrated my relationships, goals, and self-worth.

What I came to realize over time was that the trauma of war and the separation from my tribe and sense of purpose had reopened the primary wounds of childhood. These wounds—feelings of abandonment, insecurity, and unworthiness—had remained dormant until my experiences in the military and subsequent transition reignited them. I was carrying "soul contracts" that no longer served me, patterns of belief and behavior rooted in my past that perpetuated my pain.

For a time, I believed that resilience meant "sucking it up" and pushing forward, no matter the cost. But this mindset only deepened the cracks in my foundation. I found myself physically depleted, emotionally numb, and spiritually disconnected. It wasn't until I reached a breaking point that I realized resilience wasn't about suppressing pain—it was about confronting it, understanding it, and transforming it into strength.

The Path to Healing

My journey toward healing began with the humbling acknowledgment that I couldn't do it alone. Seeking help felt foreign and, frankly, uncomfortable, but it became a pivotal step. Therapy provided a space to process my experiences, while mindfulness practices helped me reconnect with the present moment. I learned that vulnerability wasn't a weakness—it was a gateway to growth.

I explored a variety of modalities to address the layers of trauma I carried. Shamanic soul journeying allowed me to reconnect with parts of myself I had long forgotten, reclaiming fragmented aspects of my identity. Eye Movement Desensitization and Reprocessing (EMDR) helped me to reprocess traumatic memories in a way that no longer held me captive. Cognitive Behavioral Therapy (CBT) provided tools to challenge and reframe destructive thought patterns, while Stoic philosophy gave me a framework for resilience rooted in logic, acceptance, and purposeful action. And through countless hours of meditation, I began to rewrite those old "soul contracts"—deep-seated agreements I'd unconsciously made with myself about who I was and what I deserved.

These practices helped me reprocess and release the afflictions of the past, allowing me to construct a new identity—one no longer defined by wounds but by growth and purpose. Functional medicine revealed the profound connection between gut health and mental clarity, while physical fitness became my anchor in maintaining discipline and focus. Behavioral psychology taught me how to reframe my thoughts, and regenerative agriculture—a surprising passion I discovered along the way—reminded me of nature's resilience and the importance of nurturing what sustains us.

Building a Purpose-Driven Life

Healing wasn't just about recovering from past wounds; it was about redefining my mission. I realized that the skills and lessons I'd gained—both on the battlefield and through my personal struggles—could serve others. This led me to a path of entrepreneurship, mentoring, and advocacy.

Through my work with veteran entrepreneurs and service-based businesses, I've seen firsthand how resilience can transform lives. Whether it's helping a fellow veteran launch a company or guiding a founder through the stresses of leadership, my goal has always been to empower others to harness their own resilience. The principles I've developed—rooted in holistic health, emotional intelligence, and purpose-driven leadership—are the foundation of everything I teach.

The Birth of Founder H.E.R.O

The idea for this book emerged from a desire to share the frameworks that have helped me and others navigate the complexities of life and business. *Founder H.E.R.O: The Holistic Path to Purpose Driven Success* is more than a guide; it's a reflection of my journey and a roadmap for anyone seeking to align their personal growth with their professional ambitions.

In these pages, you'll find strategies for building resilience across four pillars: mental, physical, spiritual, and environmental. You'll learn how to cultivate the mindset of a founder—one that thrives on purpose, authenticity, and intentionality. And you'll discover that success isn't just about achieving external milestones; it's about creating a life that feels meaningful, balanced, and aligned with your deepest values.

A Call to Action

As you begin this journey, I want to leave you with a simple yet powerful truth: resilience is not a destination; it's a practice. It's the sum of small, consistent actions taken in the face of adversity. It's the willingness to confront discomfort, embrace vulnerability, and strive for growth. And it's the recognition that healing—whether personal, professional, or communal—is both a challenge and a privilege.

My hope is that this book equips you with the tools, insights, and inspiration to step into your own "Founder H.E.R.O"—to lead with purpose, live with intention, and build a legacy that reflects the best of who you are. Whether you're a seasoned entrepreneur, a veteran transitioning into a new chapter, or someone seeking clarity in the chaos, know that you're not alone in this journey.

Resilience is within you. Let's embark on this path together.

Jim & Chris before hiking the Linville Gorge in NC

INTRODUCTION

The Evolution of Founder Resilience

Entrepreneurship has long been characterized by its dynamism, uncertainty, and the necessity for adaptive resilience. Traditional startup methodologies have primarily emphasized market strategy, product development, and operational scalability while often neglecting the holistic well-being of the founder. Yet, emerging research in business psychology, behavioral economics, and systems thinking suggests that a founder's success is inextricably linked to their ability to maintain balance across multiple domains of life.

This book, *Founder H.E.R.O.: The Holistic Path to Purpose-Driven Success*, seeks to bridge this gap by introducing a comprehensive system that enhances a founder's resilience across four fundamental domains: **Health, Economics, Relationships, and Opportunities (H.E.R.O).** This framework shows that success is not solely the product of cognitive horsepower or business acumen, but the ability to integrate and sustain resilience in all aspects of life.

The Genesis of Founder H.E.R.O.

The inception of this book was rooted in a foundational understanding of the "Founder Mode" concept popularized by Paul Graham's seminal essay on the subject. "Founder Mode" describes an intense period of deep work, focus, and immersion that many startup entrepreneurs experience when building their ventures. While undeniably effective in achieving short-term milestones, prolonged engagement in this mode often leads to burnout, diminished decision-making capacity, and ultimately, the collapse of promising enterprises.

Initially, this book was titled *Founder Mode: A Holistic Path to Purpose-Driven Success*, aiming to extend Graham's thesis by incorporating a framework that accounts for a founder's total well-being. However, due to a pending trademark by Airbnb on the phrase "Founder Mode," we took this as an opportunity to refine our perspective and develop a more comprehensive terminology that encapsulates the essence of sustainable entrepreneurial resilience. The outcome was *Founder H.E.R.O.*, a framework that not only acknowledges the importance of deep work but also recognizes the necessity of sustaining oneself through a balanced, systematic approach.

Defining the H.E.R.O. Framework

A great acronym to capture the four domains of resilience—Health, Wealth, Career/Business, and Relationships—is **HERO**:

1. **Health** – The foundation of physical and mental well-being. Without it, sustainable success is nearly impossible. Entrepreneurs must prioritize sleep, nutrition, exercise, and mental clarity to maintain peak performance.

2. **Economics (Wealth)** – Financial stability and growth are crucial in reducing stress and increasing long-term strategic thinking. Smart financial habits allow founders to build wealth sustainably, rather than falling into cycles of scarcity-driven decision-making.

3. **Relationships** – The support system of any founder. Whether through mentorship, friendships, family, or business partnerships, meaningful relationships provide stability, guidance, and resilience against the inevitable hardships of entrepreneurship.

4. **Opportunities (Career/Business Growth)** – Thriving in business requires the ability to recognize, seize, and maximize opportunities. Founders who consistently create and capitalize on opportunities position themselves for sustainable success.

The term *HERO* resonates because it symbolizes empowerment, overcoming challenges, and striving for holistic balance across these vital areas of life. This book aims to equip founders with the tools necessary to master these four domains and sustain long-term success.

The Path Forward: Toward a More Resilient Entrepreneurial Culture

A significant motivator behind writing *Founder H.E.R.O.* is the aspiration to contribute to the evolving discourse within entrepreneurial ecosystems, particularly in accelerators such as **Y Combinator (YC)**. While YC has historically favored founders who exhibit extraordinary commitment and drive, we argue that the next evolution of successful startups will be led by **founders who embody resilience in all aspects of their lives.**

It is not enough to create a scalable product or secure a high valuation. Founders must develop the mental fortitude, financial literacy, and relational intelligence necessary to sustain both personal well-being and long-term business success. A compelling example of this principle can be observed in the **PR transformation of Mark Zuckerberg** and the subsequent rebranding of Facebook to Meta. Once perceived as a highly analytical yet emotionally detached leader, Zuckerberg has gradually reshaped his public persona to emphasize personal growth, broader societal impact, and a vision for the future—most notably through his commitment to the metaverse. This strategic shift not only helped reframe his leadership in a more relatable and holistic manner but also **contributed to increasing Meta's overall market valuation**, demonstrating that the perception of a founder's resilience, adaptability, and long-term vision directly impacts business success.

Through this book, we aim to contribute not just to the field of entrepreneurship but to **a broader cultural shift in how we define and measure success.** Just as Zuckerberg's transformation illustrated the power of integrating personal and professional evolution, we assert that the modern founder must embrace a similarly holistic approach—one that values not just innovation, but also resilience across health, wealth, relationships, and opportunity.

And Maybe… Just Maybe… This Will Get Us Into Y Combinator? 👀

We're not saying this book is our secret weapon to finally getting into **Y Combinator**… but let's just say we wouldn't mind earning some extra brownie points 😉. After all, YC loves founders who think long-term, adapt quickly, and solve real problems. *Founder H.E.R.O.* is all about giving founders the ultimate resilience playbook—something every YC startup could benefit from.

A Huge Thank You! ♥

This title change was **community-driven through Linkedin**, and we couldn't have done it without your insights, votes, and suggestions. We're beyond excited to share *Founder H.E.R.O.* and the framework to your life & organization.

As this book unfolds, each chapter will provide in-depth analyses, case studies, and actionable methods for implementing the H.E.R.O. framework. From neuroscientific insights on cognitive endurance to strategic financial planning, *Founder H.E.R.O.* is designed to be an interdisciplinary guide that merges the best of psychology, economics, and strategic foresight.

Ultimately, our goal is to equip founders with the tools necessary to **not only survive the entrepreneurial journey but to thrive holistically**. We challenge you to embark on this journey of resilience, adaptability, and purpose-driven success—because in the end, every founder has the potential to be a hero.

CHAPTER 1
HOW TO USE THIS BOOK

Whether you're an aspiring entrepreneur or an established business owner looking to thrive, this book is designed to help you navigate the unique challenges and opportunities of founding and leading a purpose-driven business. If you've ever felt overwhelmed, uncertain, or unsure of how to balance personal and business growth, you're not alone. This book will guide you step by step through a holistic framework that nurtures your mind, body, spirit, and environment — all critical elements for long-term success & what we have coined as the *4 pillars of resiliency.*

In this chapter, we'll help you understand how to use the content in the following pages so it's most effective for your journey. The tools, exercises, and strategies you'll find here aren't just theoretical — they're practical steps you can take immediately to start optimizing your health, mindset, and leadership. Additionally, we'll explore parallels to the enduring principles found in other literature, and why the framework taught in this book should become a foundational part of not just your entrepreneurial library, but more importantly your personal development encyclopedia.

Navigating Your Journey: Personal and Business Success

The road to success as a founder is rarely linear. In fact, it often feels like a rollercoaster ride of highs and lows. One moment you might feel on top of the world, and the next, you're battling exhaustion, stress, or self-doubt. This book doesn't shy away from the reality of the founder's journey — it embraces it. First off though, let's start out by defining what a founder even is!

What is a Founder?

In the context of this book, a founder is more than just someone who starts a business; they are a visionary, a builder, and a leader driven by purpose. Founders don't just create products or services—they craft solutions that align with their personal values, inspire others, and contribute to a larger mission. This book views founders as individuals who take ownership of their growth, both personal and professional, recognizing that the success of their business is deeply intertwined with their well-being, mindset, and ability to lead with intention. Founders are the architects of their entrepreneurial journey, and this book equips them with the tools to navigate challenges, foster resilience, and amplify their impact.

What is a Founder Around the World?

The word **"founder"** carries a deep and universal significance across cultures, languages, and historical contexts. At its core, a founder is someone who initiates, builds, and establishes something new—whether it be a business, an institution, a movement, or a lasting legacy. However, the way different societies define and interpret the term reveals important cultural values and perspectives on leadership, creation, and long-term impact.

Global Definitions of a Founder

Across the world, various definitions of "founder" share common themes while reflecting unique cultural nuances:

- **Merriam-Webster Dictionary (USA):** "One that founds or establishes."
- **Oxford English Dictionary (UK):** "A person who establishes an institution, company, or settlement."
- **Confucian Perspective (China):** "A person who lays the moral and structural foundation of an enduring system, ensuring harmony and order."
- **Japanese Business Culture:** "A visionary who creates a lasting enterprise, embodying the principle of *kaizen* (continuous improvement)."
- **Swahili (East Africa):** *Mwanzilishi* – "One who initiates something new, bringing a legacy to the community."
- **Indigenous Māori Perspective (New Zealand):** "A guardian of creation, setting forth a path for future generations to follow."
- **Indian Entrepreneurship (Hindi: संस्थापक):** "A pioneer who transforms an idea into reality, creating opportunities for others."
- **French Perspective:** *Fondateur* – "A person who initiates and solidifies the groundwork for an enduring legacy."
- **Arabic Definition (مؤسس):** «One who builds a foundation, whether in knowledge, business, or faith, setting the stage for growth.»
- **Latin Origin:** *Fundātor* – «He who lays the base or ground, giving strength to future structures.»

Common Themes in the Definition of a Founder

From these diverse interpretations, three key themes emerge that define what it means to be a founder:

1. Creation & Establishment

A founder is, first and foremost, a **creator**—someone who takes an idea, a vision, or a purpose and transforms it into reality. Whether it's starting a company (Oxford, Japanese), building an institution (Merriam-Webster, French), or initiating a cultural movement (Swahili, Māori), founders act as **pioneers** who set things in motion.

2. Foundation & Structure

The root of the word "founder" comes from the Latin *fundātor*, meaning **one who lays a foundation**. This concept appears repeatedly in definitions that highlight **stability, order, and groundwork**—whether in business (Indian, French), philosophy (Confucian), or broader societal frameworks (Arabic). A founder does not just start something; they build it on a strong foundation to ensure longevity.

3. Legacy & Impact

Being a founder is not just about creating something—it's about leaving a **lasting mark**. Many cultures emphasize the long-term significance of founders, whether through **guiding future generations** (Māori), **continuous improvement** (*kaizen* in Japanese), or **ensuring sustainable growth** (Indian, Arabic). Founders are not just initiators; they are **architects of the future**.

While the definition of "founder" varies across cultures, the essence remains the same: a founder is someone who **creates, structures, and leaves a legacy**. They are not just individuals who start things—they are visionaries who shape the future through their actions, ensuring that what they build stands the test of time.

What Makes This Approach Unique?

Traditional business advice tends to focus on strategy, operations, and management — often overlooking the personal well-being of the founder. However, research consistently shows that personal well-being and business success are inextricably linked. A 2022 study published in the *Journal of Occupational Health Psychology* found that entrepreneurs who prioritized physical and mental health were 31% more likely to experience sustained business growth over five years compared to those who didn't.

Founder H.E.R.O is built on the premise that the health, resilience, and mindset of the founder are directly tied to the success of the business. If you're not at your best, your company won't be either. Throughout this book, you'll explore how to:

- Align your purpose with your company's mission, so every decision you make is fueled by passion and clarity.
- Develop mental and emotional resilience, helping you bounce back from setbacks and stay focused on your goals.
- Enhance your physical and spiritual well-being, ensuring you have the energy, clarity, and motivation to lead with purpose.
- Curate an environment — both physical and social — that nurtures your growth and supports your journey.

Setting Expectations and Goals

Before you dive into the content, it's important to set expectations and clarify what you hope to achieve by reading this book. Think of this as your roadmap. If you don't yet know where you're headed, this book will help you define your direction. If you already have a clear vision, it will provide the tools to get you there with greater ease and efficiency.

Questions to Guide Your Journey:

1. **What is your "Founder H.E.R.O" vision?** Are you currently in Founder Mode, or do you operate more in Manager Mode? This book will help you transition to a more holistic, purpose-driven approach to leadership.
2. **What areas of your personal life need the most attention?** Perhaps it's physical health, emotional resilience, or mental focus. Pinpoint the areas you want to improve.
3. **What business outcomes do you desire?** Do you want to scale, improve profitability, increase team engagement, or enhance your work-life balance? Clarifying these outcomes will help you track your progress.

How to Approach This Book

The holistic approach laid out in this book is designed to be practical, flexible, and actionable. Here's how you can get the most out of the content:

1. Read with Intent

As you read, take time to reflect on how each concept applies to your life and business. Don't rush through the chapters; instead, digest and implement the advice provided. Research by the *American Psychological Association* highlights the value of reflective practice, noting that leaders who engage in regular reflection improve decision-making by 23%. If you've ever read or listened to any of Alex Hormozi's books then you know that listening to the content while actively reading (with a pen to take notes) supercharges your retention.

2. Implement as You Go

Each chapter provides actionable insights and exercises. Try not to overwhelm yourself by implementing everything at once. Start with one or two key changes, and build from there.

3. Personalize the Journey

Every founder's path is unique. Adapt the tools and frameworks to work for you. According to a study in the *Harvard Business Review*, personalized strategies lead to a 27% higher rate of goal achievement.

4. Leverage Worksheets and Exercises

Use the exercises provided in each chapter to apply what you've learned in real time. These practical tools are designed to turn knowledge into action, increasing the likelihood of long-term success.

5. Track Your Progress

Keep track of your progress by journaling or creating metrics that measure improvements in your resilience, focus, and business outcomes. Small wins compound over time. As Napoleon Hill famously wrote, "Strength and growth come only through continuous effort and struggle."

A Modern Inspiration from *Think and Grow Rich*

Napoleon Hill's *Think and Grow Rich* is often regarded as one of the most influential personal development books ever written. Its principles have helped countless entrepreneurs harness the power of mindset and persistence to achieve success. Similarly, this book provides a structured, actionable framework to integrate purpose, resilience, and leadership into your entrepreneurial journey.

Here's why both books complement each other:

1. **Shared Emphasis on Purpose**: Hill's principle of "Definiteness of Purpose" aligns closely with this book's focus on mission-driven leadership. Purpose is the compass that guides all decisions.
2. **Practical Application**: While Hill focuses on visualization and mindset, this book adds actionable tools to improve your physical, mental, and emotional resilience.
3. **Timeless Principles**: Just as Hill's principles remain relevant decades after publication, the strategies in this book are designed for long-term applicability.

In John Strelecy's Sequel to the "Big Five For Life" there's a conversation about the topic of excellence over imperfection, and that is exactly how you should approach implementing the topics & strategies in this book to any aspects of your lives. The conversation goes like this "Build it right, build it beautifully, make every line, every component the right one....Yet I also realize one of the biggest mistakes people make when they build, is they build systems with the goal of excellence. All life has imperfections. There's no way around that. So better to pick the imperfections you prefer, so you can manage them on your terms, than to have the unexpected imperfections show up unexpectedly." Take these lessons in this book & apply them to your own life. Imperfect action over everything!

The Founder H.E.R.O. Plan: A Practical Framework for Resilience and Success

Introduction to Your H.E.R.O. Plan

To truly embody the Founder H.E.R.O. framework, you need a structured yet flexible approach to integrating resilience into your daily life. This plan will help you identify your top five priorities within each of the four H.E.R.O. domains—Health, Economics (Wealth), Relationships, and Opportunities—and then narrow them down to the single most critical focus area in each category. By doing so, you will create a personalized, actionable strategy for sustained success.

Step 1: Define Your Top 5 Priorities in Each H.E.R.O. Domain

Take a moment to reflect on your current strengths, weaknesses, and areas for growth. Below, list your top five priorities for each domain, focusing on what will most significantly impact your personal and business success.

Health (Physical & Mental Well-being)

1. _____
2. _____
3. _____
4. _____
5. _____

Example: Prioritizing sleep, daily exercise, stress management, balanced nutrition, and mental clarity through meditation.

Economics (Wealth Resilience & Financial Stability)

1. _____
2. _____
3. _____
4. _____
5. _____

Example: Increasing cash flow, reducing debt, diversifying investments, improving financial literacy, and leveraging Bitcoin for long-term financial security.

Relationships (Personal & Professional Network)

1. _____
2. _____
3. _____
4. _____
5. _____

Example: Strengthening family bonds, networking with mentors, improving communication skills, deepening business partnerships, and engaging in community support.

Opportunities (Business & Career Growth)

1. _____
2. _____
3. _____

4. _____
5. _____

Example: Expanding market reach, developing new products, improving leadership skills, leveraging emerging technologies, and mastering digital marketing strategies.

Step 2: Select Your #1 Priority in Each Domain

From your top five, select the **single most important focus area** in each category that will drive the greatest long-term impact.

- **Health Priority:** _____
- **Economics Priority:** _____
- **Relationships Priority:** _____
- **Opportunities Priority:** _____

By focusing on these four key areas, you will build a resilient foundation for both personal and business success.

The 4 Drivers of Resilience

Just as John Strelecky's *Big Five for Life* helps individuals align their daily actions with their life's purpose, the *Four Drivers of Resilience* serve as foundational pillars that ensure stability, adaptability, and success in both business and life. Strelecky's framework encourages people to define five key things they want to achieve in their lifetime, shaping their decisions and priorities. Similarly, the Four Drivers of Resilience—Health, Economics, Relationships, and Opportunities—help founders and entrepreneurs build a strong, adaptable foundation for sustainable growth and well-being.

Each of these four drivers plays a critical role:

- **Health:** The core of personal resilience—physical and mental well-being enable peak performance and longevity.
- **Economics:** Financial resilience ensures long-term stability and the freedom to navigate challenges.
- **Relationships:** A strong network provides emotional support, business connections, and collaborative growth.
- **Opportunities:** Growth, innovation, and continuous learning open doors to new ventures and personal fulfillment.

By prioritizing these drivers, you align your actions with long-term success, just as the *Big Five for Life* framework encourages intentionality in personal fulfillment.

Step 3: Implement & Track Your Progress

Actionable Steps for Each Priority

For each selected priority, outline three actionable steps you will take over the next 30 days to make progress.

Health: (Example: If your priority is improving sleep)

1. Set a consistent bedtime and wake-up schedule.
2. Reduce screen time before bed.
3. Establish a relaxing nighttime routine (reading, journaling, meditation, etc.).

Economics: (Example: If your priority is increasing cash flow)

1. Identify unnecessary expenses and cut costs.

2. Increase revenue streams through new business initiatives.
3. Automate savings and investments.

Relationships: (Example: If your priority is strengthening professional connections)

1. Schedule weekly check-ins with key mentors or advisors.
2. Attend industry networking events.
3. Improve communication skills through coaching or practice.

Opportunities: (Example: If your priority is expanding market reach)

1. Develop a content marketing strategy.
2. Conduct market research to identify new customer segments.
3. Invest in business development and outreach initiatives.

Founder's Commitment

Resilience isn't built overnight—it's cultivated through intentional action, consistency, and adaptability. By following the H.E.R.O. Plan, you create a structured yet flexible strategy to balance personal well-being and business success.

Your Commitment Statement:

"I commit to prioritizing my health, financial resilience, relationships, and opportunities in a balanced and sustainable way. I will take intentional action daily to build the life and business I envision."

Sign & Date: _____ | ____-____-_____ .

Your Next Steps

- Set a reminder to review and adjust your H.E.R.O. Plan in 30 days.
- Keep this document accessible and revisit it weekly for accountability.
- Share your goals with an accountability partner, mentor, or mastermind group.

CHAPTER 2
INTRODUCTION TO FOUNDER MODE

What is Founder Mode?

In the world of business, founders often wear many hats. From the visionary who creates the idea, to the leader who assembles a team, to the strategist who grows the company — a founder is a multifaceted role. But what does it really mean to be in Founder Mode? Simply put, **Founder Mode** is the mindset and approach that integrates your personal purpose with your business. It's a state where you lead not just from a place of strategy or management, but from a deeper alignment between your vision and your values.

Founder Mode is not just about growing a business — it's about becoming the kind of leader who embodies resilience, creativity, and authenticity in every decision. It's about living your purpose every day, and letting that purpose drive everything you do, from how you manage your team to how you navigate challenges. It's more than leadership; it's a holistic approach that considers who you are as a person and how that impacts your business.

Founder Mode vs. Manager Mode

Many founders start out as passionate entrepreneurs, driven by an idea, a mission, or a vision for the world. But as the company grows, many are pressured to take on a more managerial role, focusing more on day-to-day operations, managing teams, and overseeing processes. This is what we refer to as **Manager Mode**.

In Manager Mode, a founder often becomes disconnected from the very essence of why they started the business. They may get bogged down in tasks that drain energy, such as micromanaging employees, managing financial spreadsheets, or dealing with endless emails and meetings. While management skills are undeniably important, they aren't the heart of what makes a business truly thrive. What differentiates Founder Mode from Manager Mode is the focus on leadership that stems from a clear vision and deep personal commitment, rather than purely operational tasks.

Key Differences Between Founder Mode and Manager Mode:

Founder Mode	Manager Mode
Focuses on big-picture vision, purpose, and values.	Focuses on day-to-day operations, processes, and logistics.
Leads with creativity, authenticity, and passion.	Leads with structure, oversight, and control.
Empowers others to execute, rather than micromanaging.	Handles most tasks themselves, limiting delegation.

Embraces adaptability, innovation, and long-term thinking.	Follows established procedures and norms.
Prioritizes personal growth alongside business growth.	Prioritizes business continuity and immediate concerns over long-term growth.

While both modes have their place, the challenge for many founders is balancing these modes without sacrificing their core mission. **Founder Mode** is about leading with purpose, allowing you to scale your business without losing your authentic self or the vision that started it all.

Why Traditional Management Advice Fails Founders

Many founders turn to traditional business advice or management books for solutions to their challenges. The problem is, much of this advice is designed for managers who are overseeing established companies with established structures, not the high-energy, fluid, and purpose-driven approach needed for founders. The emphasis is often placed on operations, numbers, and delegation, with little regard for the mental, emotional, and spiritual well-being of the founders themselves.

Here's where traditional management advice often misses the mark for founders:

- **Lack of Personal Alignment**: Traditional advice doesn't address the deep connection between a founder's personal values and the company's mission. Founders who don't integrate these aspects can easily burn out or feel disconnected from their businesses, leading to poor decision-making and stress.

- **Focus on Control, Not Empowerment**: Traditional management often emphasizes control over creative freedom. Founders, however, thrive on innovation and autonomy, both in themselves and their teams. A rigid, top-down structure can stifle the creativity that fueled their original vision.
- **Burnout and Well-being**: Founders are often told to "work harder, hustle more." This mindset, while it may lead to short-term success, overlooks the importance of resilience, self-care, and mental well-being. Without these elements, a founder's energy will deplete, negatively impacting both themselves and their business.

By embracing **Founder Mode**, you shift your focus from "getting things done" to "leading with purpose," allowing your business to evolve naturally without losing touch with your deeper mission. It's about setting yourself and your company up for sustainable growth — both professionally and personally.

Founder Mode in Action: The Power of Personal Alignment

To truly understand Founder Mode, let's explore a key insight shared by Paul Graham, co-founder of Y Combinator, based on his experience with some of the most successful entrepreneurs in Silicon Valley. In a talk given by Brian Chesky, the CEO of Airbnb, Graham observed a fundamental distinction between how founders run their companies and how professional managers do.

Graham's key takeaway was that **scaling a startup does not require shifting from founder mode to manager mode**. While traditional wisdom holds that as a company grows, the founder should take a step back and let professional managers handle the day-to-day operations, this approach often backfires. Founders who try to follow this conventional advice may feel increasingly disconnected from their vision, and their companies may suffer as a result.

Brian Chesky's personal experience aligns with Graham's insights. Chesky discovered that trying to follow traditional advice about running Airbnb, such as hiring good people and giving them room to do their jobs, led to disastrous results. Instead, he found that maintaining a **"founder's touch"** — staying involved in the company's culture and vision — was essential for its success. In fact, Chesky turned to studying Steve Jobs' management style, particularly his ability to maintain a visionary presence within Apple, even as the company scaled.

What Graham and Chesky illustrate is the profound difference between **Founder Mode** and **Manager Mode**. While Manager Mode may work for established businesses with structured hierarchies, it's often too rigid and formulaic for fast-growing startups. The heart of **Founder Mode** lies in **personal alignment** — the connection between the founder's deep sense of purpose and the company's mission. This alignment fuels creativity, fosters innovation, and ensures that the founder stays connected to their vision even as the company expands.

Shifting Focus to Founder H.E.R.O & the Power of Purpose-Driven Leadership

One of the core pillars of **Founder H.E.R.O** is **purpose-driven leadership**. When you operate from a place of purpose, you become a magnetic force that attracts like-minded individuals, opportunities, and success. Purpose-driven leadership allows you to:

- **Inspire Others**: People naturally want to follow leaders who have a clear sense of why they do what they do. When you lead with purpose, you inspire your team to believe in your vision, and they become more invested in the success of the company.

- **Navigate Challenges with Resilience**: Every business will face setbacks. With a strong sense of purpose, you can navigate these challenges with resilience, knowing that your deeper mission is guiding you through tough times.

- **Create Long-Term Impact**: Purpose-driven leadership isn't just about short-term profits. It's about creating something lasting, something meaningful. It's about shaping an organization that is aligned with your core values, which attracts customers, investors, and employees who share your beliefs.

By consistently aligning your personal values with the mission of your business, you'll be able to stay motivated, focused, and energized, even when the going gets tough. You'll be leading from a place of deep conviction, not just reacting to challenges as they arise. This creates a powerful foundation for growth that's sustainable over the long term.

The Role of Purpose in Business Success

At the core of the **Founder H.E.R.O Framework** is the understanding that personal fulfillment and business success are deeply intertwined. When you're aligned with your purpose, your business doesn't just succeed financially — it also becomes a source of meaning and fulfillment. This leads to:

- **Enhanced Creativity and Innovation**: When your work is aligned with your purpose, you are more likely to think creatively and come up with innovative solutions. This creativity is essential for growing your business in unique and sustainable ways.

- **Greater Resilience**: A purpose-driven founder can face setbacks with resilience. Knowing why you started your business and staying connected to that purpose helps you keep going, even when challenges arise.

- **Attraction of Like-minded Partners**: Purpose-driven leadership draws people who share your values. Whether it's investors, employees, or customers, people are naturally drawn to businesses with a clear, authentic purpose that aligns with their own beliefs.

By operating in **Founder H.E.R.O**, you create a powerful feedback loop between personal growth and business growth. As your company evolves, you don't lose sight of why you started in the first place — your mission remains clear, and your purpose-driven leadership becomes the catalyst for both personal and professional success.

Now, let's explore how to tap into your purpose and unlock your full potential as a leader. By connecting your personal values with your business vision, you'll create the foundation for a lasting impact, transforming not just your company, but the world around you.

Founder HERO Actionable Worksheet

Step 1: Define Your Personal Purpose

To operate in Founder Mode, you must align your personal purpose with your business vision. Use the prompts below to clarify your core purpose.

1. **What drives you?** (Why did you start your business? What impact do you want to create?)

- _____
- _____

2. **What core values define you as a leader?** (List at least three values that shape your decision-making.)

    - _____
    - _____
    - _____

3. **How do you want to be remembered as a founder?** (Describe your legacy and long-term vision.)

    - _____
    - _____
    - _____

Step 2: Identify Founder Mode vs. Manager Mode Tendencies

Reflect on your leadership habits to determine if you are operating in Founder Mode or slipping into Manager Mode.

Where do you spend most of your time?

How do you lead your team?

How do you handle challenges?

Step 3: Re-align Your Leadership Approach

For any area where you identified Manager Mode tendencies, write down an action you will take to shift towards Founder Mode.

1. **If I am too focused on operations, I will:**

    - _____

2. **If I find myself micromanaging, I will:**

   - _____

3. **If I struggle with innovation and adaptability, I will:**

   - _____

Step 4: Apply Purpose-Driven Leadership

To reinforce your alignment with Founder Mode, use these prompts to create an action plan.

1. **What is one decision I can make today that aligns with my purpose?**

   - _____

2. **How can I better inspire my team and communicate my vision?**

   - _____

3. **What is one way I can prioritize my personal growth alongside business growth?**

   - _____

Step 5: Founder Mode Commitment Statement

Fill in the blanks to solidify your commitment to Founder Mode.

"I commit to leading my business with **[core value]**, **[core value]**, and **[core value]**. I will focus on **[big-picture goal]** and inspire my team by **[leadership action]**. By aligning my purpose with my business, I will create a lasting impact and ensure both personal and professional growth."

Sign & Date: _____ | ____-____-_____.

CHAPTER 3
THE FOUNDER'S MINDSET

Initially when writing this book we introduced the word 'Resilience' under the assumption that anyone that reads this will ultimately know what resilience really means. We decided to add this lesson on defining resilience and the pillars to better improve your understanding on how applying resilience to your life could make or break your success as a founder.

What is Resilience?

Resilience is the process of negotiating, managing, and adapting to significant sources of stress or trauma. It is facilitated by assets and resources within the individual, their life, and environment, enabling them to "bounce back" in the face of adversity. However, the experience of resilience varies across the life course.

> **Definition:** "Resilience is the process of negotiating, managing and adapting to significant sources of stress or trauma. Assets and resources within the individual, their life and environment facilitate this capacity for adaptation and 'bouncing back' in the face of adversity. Across the life course, the experience of resilience will vary." — Usher K, et al. (2021)

Two Paths in Response to Adversity

When faced with adversity, individuals often take one of two primary paths:

Path 1: Growth and Adaptation (Post-Traumatic Growth)

Characteristics:

- **Learning:** Using the experience as an opportunity for self-discovery and personal growth.
- **Resilience:** Building mental and emotional strength to better handle future challenges.
- **Acceptance:** Acknowledging the reality of the situation and finding ways to move forward.
- **Re-evaluation of Priorities:** Recognizing what truly matters and shifting life goals.
- **Empathy:** Developing deeper understanding and compassion for others facing challenges.

Outcomes: Individuals can emerge stronger and better equipped to handle future challenges, often gaining a renewed sense of purpose, improved relationships, or a deeper appreciation for life.

Path 2: Dysfunction and Maladaptation

Characteristics:

- **Avoidance:** Denying the reality of the situation or using unhealthy coping mechanisms.
- **Chronic Stress:** Persistent feelings of being overwhelmed, leading to physical and mental health issues.
- **Victim Mentality:** Believing one has no control over life circumstances.

- **Isolation:** Withdrawing from social connections and support systems.

Outcomes: Prolonged suffering, mental health issues like depression or anxiety, physical health problems, or strained relationships. This path can exacerbate challenges during future adversities.

As an entrepreneur, the demands of **Founder H.E.R.O** are relentless. From making critical business decisions to managing personal obligations, founders face a unique mix of challenges that test their physical, emotional, and mental limits daily. In such an environment, resilience isn't just a desirable trait; it's a necessity. Dividing resilience into the four domains of **Health, Wealth, Career/Business, and Relationships** provides a structured framework to build, sustain, and optimize this critical attribute. Formerly known as H.E.R.O. Here's why this approach is exceptionally beneficial for founders:

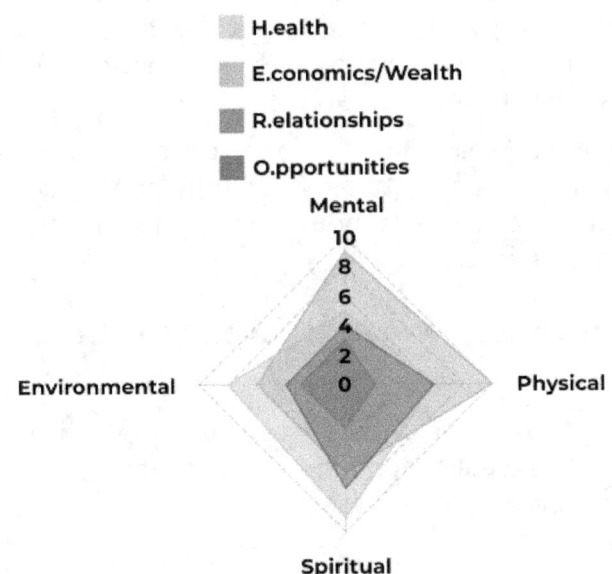

This spider chart provides a great visual representation of the four domains of resilience and how mental, physical, spiritual and environmental factors impact each area of our lives both personally and professionally.

1. Health: The Foundation of Founder Resilience

A founder's energy and clarity are directly tied to their physical and mental health. Entrepreneurs are often guilty of sacrificing sleep, proper nutrition, and mental health for the sake of their ventures. However, prioritizing the **health domain** ensures that the foundation of resilience is strong.

- **Physical Well-being:** Regular exercise and a balanced diet enhance energy levels, boost cognitive function, and increase stamina for long workdays. Founders who maintain their physical health can sustain the intensity required to build and scale a business.
- **Mental and Emotional Well-being:** Startups are fraught with uncertainty, and stress is a constant companion. Developing tools like mindfulness, therapy, or stress management techniques equips founders to navigate crises with calm and clarity.
- **Spiritual Well-being:** Purpose-driven entrepreneurs find that grounding their work in personal values or a higher mission fuels motivation and provides a sense of peace amidst chaos.

2. (Economics) - Wealth: Beyond the Bottom Line

For founders, financial stability extends beyond personal security. The **wealth domain** serves as a measure of both personal and business resilience.

- **Security:** Having a financial buffer allows entrepreneurs to take calculated risks without jeopardizing personal or business viability. It reduces stress and enables decision-making from a position of strength rather than desperation.
- **Opportunities:** Access to capital can open doors to partnerships, marketing campaigns, and scaling initiatives that drive business growth. For founders, financial resilience directly correlates with the ability to seize pivotal opportunities.
- **Legacy:** Building wealth as a founder isn't just about profits—it's about creating value, leaving an impact, and securing a future for both the business and personal causes close to your heart.

3. Relationships: The Unseen Startup Fuel

In the high-stakes world of startups, it's easy to neglect personal relationships. However, the **relationships domain** is vital for maintaining long-term resilience.

- **Emotional Support:** Founders often face moments of doubt and isolation. Having a strong support system—whether it's family, friends, or mentors—provides the emotional grounding needed to stay the course.
- **Personal Growth:** Relationships challenge founders to grow emotionally, offering insights and perspectives that improve leadership and interpersonal skills critical for building a team and managing stakeholders.
- **Social Network:** Networking isn't just about business—it's about building meaningful connections. A founder's social circle often provides resources, ideas, and opportunities that drive both personal and business success.

4. (Opportunities) - Career/Business: Purpose Meets Performance

Founders inherently live in the **career/business domain**, but thriving in this area requires aligning professional goals with personal resilience.

- **Personal Fulfillment:** Running a startup can be a grind, but aligning business goals with personal passions ensures that the journey remains rewarding. Founders who derive meaning from their work are less likely to burn out.
- **Social Impact:** Entrepreneurs have the unique opportunity to create change through their ventures. Connecting their work to a greater good amplifies resilience by infusing a sense of purpose.
- **Financial Support:** A successful business becomes a self-sustaining engine that not only supports the founder's lifestyle but also reinforces the wealth domain, enabling further personal and professional growth.

Why This Framework Works for Founders

The act of dividing resilience into these domains gives founders a clear, actionable map to address the multifaceted challenges of entrepreneurship. It prevents the overwhelm that comes from trying to "do it all" by encouraging strategic focus on distinct areas.

- **Holistic Growth:** By balancing these domains, founders avoid over-prioritizing one area—like business success—at the expense of others, such as health or relationships.
- **Measurable Progress:** Breaking resilience into specific domains makes it easier to set goals, track progress, and identify areas needing attention.

- **Sustainable Success:** Long-term business success is built on personal sustainability. Addressing these domains ensures founders remain resilient not just for months, but for years.

In the high-pressure world of being in a founder's mindset, resilience isn't just about surviving—it's about thriving. Embracing these four domains ensures that entrepreneurs can weather the challenges, seize the opportunities, and build not only successful businesses but also fulfilling lives.

Leveraging Neuroplasticity to Overcome Challenges

The journey of a founder is full of challenges, setbacks, and moments of doubt. But at the core of every successful founder is something essential: resilience. Resilience isn't just about bouncing back from difficulties — it's about cultivating the mental toughness to not only endure hardships but to use them as stepping stones for growth.

As a founder, you will inevitably face obstacles, whether it's navigating the uncertainty of the startup world, dealing with financial stress, or leading a team through difficult times. The key to thriving through these challenges is not in avoiding them, but in developing the resilience to handle them effectively.

One of the most powerful ways to build resilience is by understanding and leveraging the concept of neuroplasticity — the brain's ability to reorganize itself by forming new neural connections throughout life. When you understand that your brain is capable of growth and adaptation, you realize that mental toughness is a skill that can be developed over time. This means that resilience isn't a fixed trait — it's something you can train and strengthen, just like physical muscles.

The ability to bounce back from failure and stay the course is what distinguishes successful founders from those who give up too soon. This is where **Founder H.E.R.O** makes a difference — it's about seeing each obstacle not as a roadblock but as a part of the journey, a moment to grow and learn.

Stoic Philosophy and Character Development

Cultivating Virtue "The Highest Good"

The Stoics believed that every situation we confront in life is an opportunity to demonstrate virtuous behavior.

Dichotomy of Control

Social Learning Theory, developed by psychologist Julian Rotter (1954) describes what he called the "Locus of Control" which refers to an individual's perception about the underlying main causes of events in his/her life. Said more simply, Do they believe that the events that unfold in their life are controlled by external forces (god, fate, luck, others), that they are just merely a product of circumstance or are they the ones in control. This can be broken down into two ends of a spectrum:

- **Internal**
    - Individuals believe that their behavior is guided by their personal decisions and effort. (personal accountability)
    - It is generally considered healthy to feel as if you are in control of your actions, behaviors, and outcomes.
    - Can be good or bad. Internal locus of control must be paired with competence and self efficacy in or-

der to result in the kinds of desirable outcomes we hope to achieve from our efforts. Without competence, over emphasis on internal control can lead to depression, anxious or neurotic behavior.
  - Tend to be higher achievers
  - This is a skill that can be taught, or learned meaning that one's LOC is a response to past experiences.

- **External**
  - Individuals believe their behavior is guided by fate, luck or other external circumstances. E.g. I did well on the exam because it was easy vs because I was prepared. Or She said I look nice because of the lighting vs. because I actually do look really nice.
  - As you can see from that last example, this inner voice, or self-talk can become our own internal narrative that we tell ourselves which ultimately plays out in our lives.

Wisdom

The Stoics believed that wisdom can help us to divide life into three separate categories:

- **Good**- Also known as acting with virtue. Some stoics believed that virtuous behavior and decisions were the only good and everything else was bad or indifferent. Good can be demonstrated as moderation, empathy, discipline, grace.
- **Bad-** Anything not virtuous, such as lying, cheating, laziness, meanness, greed.
- **Indifferent-** Anything that could be used for good or bad such as money, recognition, physical fitness, social status. All of these things could be good or bad, depending on the reason behind them.

> "The chief task in life is simply this: to identify and separate matters so that I can say clearly to myself which are externals not under my control, and which have to do with the choices I actually control. Where then do I look for good and evil? Not to uncontrollable externals, but within myself to the choices that are my own"
> **- Epictetus, Discourses, 2.5.4–5**

Courage

- The opposite of cowardice
- Not the elimination of fear, desire or anxiety, rather it is the right action despite them.
- Standing up for what is right
- Taking challenges head on without becoming overwhelmed by fear.

> "There are misfortunes which strike the sage – without incapacitating him, of course – such as physical pain, infirmity, the loss of friends or children, or the catastrophes of his country when it is devastated by war. I grant that he is sensitive to these things, for we do not impute to him the hardness of a rock or of iron. There is no virtue in putting up with that which one does not feel."
> **-Seneca**

This passage by Seneca describes how if you don't have the courage to address feelings that threaten cowardice and fear in the first place, then you cannot conquer it. Essentially, this leads us to understand that to be vulnerable is to be courageous.

By selecting for the ability to remain vulnerable even when it's scary or we don't want to is a significant step in your personal journey of growth and healing that will impact literally every aspect of your life.

Let's face it, building something from the ground up is no small feat. You're juggling tasks, battling doubt, and trying to keep your sanity intact. But what if I told you that ancient Stoic wisdom could be your secret weapon? Let's dive into two powerful Stoic principles: Justice and Temperance, and how they can transform not just your business but your life.

Justice: The Ultimate Team Player Mindset

Justice isn't just about what's fair in a court of law—it's about how we treat each other every single day. Imagine a world where everyone followed the golden rule: treat others how you'd want to be treated. Sounds like a utopia, right? Well, Marcus Aurelius thought so too.

He said, "And a commitment to justice in your own acts. Which means: thought and action resulting in the common good. What you were born to do." In simpler terms, being just is about contributing to the greater good, not just your personal gain.

Here's the kicker: justice in business means being the kind of leader who lifts others up. Celebrate your team's wins as if they were your own. Because guess what? They are. Your success is intertwined with theirs. Seneca nailed it when he wrote, "It's in keeping with Nature to show our friends affection and to celebrate their advancement, as if it were our very own."

So, the next time your teammate hits a milestone or a colleague nails that big presentation, celebrate it like you would your own victory. This isn't just good karma; it's good business.

Temperance: Mastering the Art of Enough

Now, onto Temperance, or as I like to call it, the art of "knowing when to say when." In the startup world, it's easy to get caught up in the hustle culture—late nights, endless coffee, and the constant grind. But Stoics warn against this hedonistic trap.

Seneca gives us a reality check: "Until we have begun to go without them, we fail to realize how unnecessary many things are. We've been using them not because we needed them but because we had them." Think about it—how often do we chase things we don't really need just because they're there? That latest gadget, the fancy office space, or even that extra cup of coffee.

Temperance teaches us to pause, reflect, and ask, "Do I really need this?" It's about finding balance, not just in your personal desires but in how you run your business. Overindulgence isn't just about physical pleasures; it's about overcommitting, overexpanding, and overthinking.

Marcus Aurelius offers a guiding star: "If, at some point in your life, you should come across anything better than justice, prudence, self-control, courage... if you find anything better than that, embrace it without reservations." Spoiler alert: you probably won't find anything better. So, stick to the basics—justice, self-control, and courage—and you'll be just fine.

Embracing Adversity

The obstacle is the way: Our ability to face life's challenges with grit, and determination with a smile on our face largely depends on the way we view the situation and ourselves. Our attitude towards our locus of control, and virtue are useful predictors of how we will manage stress when facing adversity.

- Perception determines impact on you
    - If you feel helpless, then you will be.
- Worry about yourself
    - Focus on what you have control over and let go of the rest
- Struggle breeds greatness
    - Failure and challenge enable us to develop the skills necessary to make achieving long term goals possible.

    *Hint: If it's anything worth doing, it will take at least a decade to master or even start getting "good"

Practicing Detachment

From distractions:

Make the most of your time. By learning to take advantage of your most productive hours with effective time management strategies and limit distractions during those times. ie. social media, email, phone calls, texts, etc.

From outcomes:

In order to maintain the focus and clarity that you need to effectively work through problems in work, relationships or otherwise we must learn to detach ourselves, our value, self worth or our opinions from the outcome of said action.

From the problem:

In his book, *The Obstacle is the Way*, Ryan Holiday shares tips on how to manage your perspective and remain objective when trying to solve problems. One approach is to remove yourself from the scenario. Pretend you are advising someone else on the problem. What are all the ways someone might solve this challenge?

Developing Mental Toughness Through Stoic Philosophy

One of the most powerful schools of thought for developing resilience is *Stoic philosophy*. Stoicism, which has been practiced by great leaders and thinkers throughout history, emphasizes the importance of controlling what you can control and letting go of what you can't. For founders, this mindset is invaluable.

The Stoic Approach to Leadership

- **Focus on What You Can Control:** As a founder, you can't control everything — especially external factors like market fluctuations, competition, or even personal challenges. However, you do have control over your responses to these situations. Stoicism teaches you to focus your energy on what you can change and to accept what you cannot.

- **Develop Emotional Mastery:** Stoicism encourages emotional discipline. As a founder, it's easy to get swept up in highs and lows. Stoics emphasize the practice of maintaining emotional balance, regardless of external circumstances. By managing your emotions, you can think more clearly, make better decisions, and lead your team with confidence.

- **Embrace Adversity as a Teacher:** Stoics view challenges and adversity not as threats but as opportunities to learn and grow. This mindset allows you to face difficult situations with the understanding that they are helping you become a better leader and a stronger person.

Practical Stoic Exercises for Founders

- **The Dichotomy of Control:** Write down the things that are within your control and those that are not. Focus your attention and energy on the former. This simple exercise helps you reframe your mindset and avoid stress over things you cannot change.

- **Daily Reflection:** Take time at the end of each day to reflect on what went well and what you could improve. This practice helps you grow mentally and emotionally by acknowledging both successes and failures as opportunities for growth.

- **Negative Visualization:** Imagine losing everything — your business, your wealth, your relationships. While this may seem counterintuitive, this Stoic exercise helps you appreciate what you have and prepare for potential setbacks without fear.

Stoicism as a Philosophy of Resilience

Stoicism is a philosophy that originated in ancient Greece and was founded by the philosopher Zeno of Citium in the early 3rd century BCE. It is a school of philosophy that emphasizes self-control, personal responsibility, and the acceptance of one's fate. The Stoics believed that a virtuous life was the key to happiness and that one should strive to live in accordance with reason and nature. This philosophy has endured for over 2,000 years and has been embraced by many as a means of coping with life's challenges and promoting resilience.

The main tenets of Stoicism include:

1. Virtue is the only good: The Stoics believed that the only thing that was truly valuable was moral virtue. They believed that material possessions, fame, and pleasure

were ultimately meaningless in the grand scheme of things.

2. Live in accordance with nature: The Stoics believed that human beings were meant to live in harmony with nature. They believed that we should accept what happens in life, focus on what we can control, and let go of what we cannot control.

3. Live in the present moment: The Stoics believed that we should focus on the present moment and not worry about the past or the future. They believed that dwelling on the past or worrying about the future only leads to anxiety and suffering.

4. Practice self-control: The Stoics believed that we should practice self-control and discipline in all aspects of our lives. They believed that this was the key to achieving inner peace and tranquility.

5. Embrace adversity: The Stoics believed that adversity was an opportunity for growth and that we should embrace it rather than resist it. They believed that facing challenges with courage and resilience was the path to personal growth and fulfillment.

Stoicism has been embraced by many as a means of promoting resilience and coping with life's challenges. One of the most famous Stoic philosophers was the Roman emperor Marcus Aurelius, who wrote extensively on the subject of Stoicism in his book Meditations. In this book, Aurelius stresses the importance of self-control, acceptance, and resilience in the face of adversity.

Stoicism has been shown to be effective in promoting resilience in a variety of contexts. For example, studies have shown that practicing Stoicism can help military personnel cope with the stress of combat and improve their mental health. It has also been shown to be effective in promoting resilience in healthcare workers who are dealing with the stress of the COVID-19 pandemic.

In conclusion, Stoicism is a philosophy that emphasizes self-control, personal responsibility, and the acceptance of one's fate. Its main tenets include the belief that virtue is the only good, that we should live in accordance with nature, and that we should embrace adversity. Stoicism has been embraced by many as a means of promoting resilience and coping with life's challenges, and has been shown to be effective in a variety of contexts.

Stoicism as an Actionable Philosophy

Stoicism is a philosophical school that teaches individuals how to deal with the adversities of life in a way that promotes resilience and inner peace. The Stoics believed that happiness comes from within and can be achieved by living in accordance with nature and practicing virtues such as wisdom, courage, self-control, and justice.

One of the key teachings of stoic philosophy is the concept of "dichotomy of control." This idea states that there are things within our control, such as our thoughts, emotions, and actions, and things outside of our control, such as the weather, other people's behavior, and external events. Stoics believe that focusing on things outside of our control leads to unnecessary stress and anxiety, and that instead, we should focus on what we can control in order to live a fulfilling and resilient life.

Stoicism also emphasizes the importance of rational thinking and objective analysis. By using reason to examine our own thoughts and emotions, we can better understand our reactions to stressors and work to eliminate sources of psychological stress in our lives. Stoics believed that negative emotions such as anger, fear, and anxiety arise from faulty reasoning and that by identifying and correcting our cognitive distortions, we can reduce their impact on our lives.

Another important aspect of stoic philosophy is the practice of "negative visualization." This involves imagining worst-case scenarios and preparing ourselves mentally and emotionally for them. By confronting our fears and anxieties in a controlled setting, we can reduce their power over us and develop a greater sense of resilience and equanimity in the face of adversity.

Stoics also believed in the importance of cultivating strong interpersonal relationships as a source of support and resilience. By valuing virtues such as kindness, compassion, and empathy, we can build meaningful connections with others that provide a sense of belonging and purpose. This social support can help us to cope with stressors and provide a sense of resilience in difficult times.

Another key component of Stoic philosophy is the idea of self-discipline. According to Stoic philosophy, self-discipline is essential for living a fulfilling life. This means that we should be mindful of our thoughts, emotions, and actions and work to cultivate positive habits that promote well-being. By developing self-discipline, we can reduce stress and promote resilience because we are better equipped to deal with challenges and setbacks.

Finally, Stoicism emphasizes the importance of community and social connections. According to Stoic philosophy, we are social creatures and need to be part of a community to thrive. By building strong relationships with others and being part of a community, we can reduce stress and promote resilience. This is because we have a support network that can help us through difficult times and provide us with a sense of belonging.

There are many practical applications of stoic philosophy in everyday life that can help to eliminate sources of psychological stress. For example, by adopting a more objective perspective on stressful events, we can avoid catastrophizing and develop a more balanced view of our situation. By practicing negative visualization, we can prepare ourselves for potential stressors and reduce their impact on our lives. By focusing on what is within our control and letting go of things outside of our control, we can reduce feelings of helplessness and promote resilience.

Research has shown that the practice of stoic philosophy can have a positive impact on mental health and well-being. A study published in the Journal of Positive Psychology found that individuals who identified as stoics reported lower levels of anxiety and depression compared to non-stoics. Another study published in the Journal of Cognitive Psychotherapy found that the use of stoic principles in cognitive-behavioral therapy (CBT) led to greater improvements in anxiety and depression symptoms compared to traditional CBT techniques.

In conclusion, Stoicism can be a powerful tool for eliminating sources of psychological stress and promoting resilience. By focusing on what is within our control, accepting things that are outside of our control, living in the present moment, developing self-discipline, and building strong relationships with others, we can reduce stress and live a more fulfilling life. Stoicism is a philosophy that has been around for centuries, and its principles are still relevant today. By adopting Stoic principles, we can cultivate resilience and thrive in the face of adversity.

How Ryan Holiday Leveraged Stoicism for Business Success

Ryan Holiday, author and founder of Brass Check Marketing, is a modern example of how Stoic philosophy can be applied to entrepreneurship. Early in his career, Holiday worked with major brands and prominent authors, but he faced intense stress, failures, and constant uncertainty. Instead of allowing these challenges to overwhelm him, Holiday turned to the teachings of ancient Stoic philosophers like Marcus Aurelius, Epictetus, and Seneca.

- **Focus on What You Can Control:** Holiday embraced the Stoic principle of focusing only on what was within his power. For instance, when faced with client rejections or business setbacks, he refused to dwell on external outcomes. Instead, he concentrated on delivering exceptional work and improving his skills.
- **Embrace Failure as Growth:** When one of his projects failed, Holiday redefined the experience as an opportunity to learn. He viewed failure not as a loss but as a necessary step toward growth and resilience.
- **Daily Stoic Practices:** Holiday developed rituals such as journaling and daily reflections to maintain clarity and emotional balance. He credits these practices for helping him manage stress and stay focused on long-term goals, regardless of immediate challenges.

Ryan Holiday's journey demonstrates that Stoicism isn't just theoretical — it's a practical toolkit for navigating the uncertainty of entrepreneurship. By mastering his mindset and focusing on what he could control, Holiday turned obstacles into stepping stones, growing both as a leader and as a business owner.

Cultivating Motivation and Stress Management Techniques

Motivation is crucial for a founder. It's what gets you out of bed in the morning and pushes you to make progress even when the road is tough. But motivation isn't a one-time burst — it needs to be cultivated and sustained over time.

Intrinsic vs. Extrinsic Motivation

As a founder, you will likely experience both intrinsic and extrinsic motivation. Intrinsic motivation comes from within — it's the passion, purpose, and drive that makes you continue working on your business. Extrinsic motivation, on the other hand, comes from external rewards such as money, recognition, or growth.

While both types of motivation can be powerful, research shows that intrinsic motivation is far more sustainable over the long term. Founders who are intrinsically motivated are more likely to stay focused on their mission and purpose, rather than becoming distracted by external pressures or short-term rewards.

Stress Management Techniques for Founders

- **Mindfulness and Meditation:** Regular mindfulness practices, such as meditation, help you stay grounded and calm amidst chaos. These practices also improve your focus and decision-making skills.
- **Breathing Exercises:** Simple deep-breathing exercises can activate the body's relaxation response, reducing stress and increasing clarity. Try deep breathing for five minutes whenever you feel overwhelmed.
- **Physical Activity:** Exercise is a powerful tool for reducing stress and increasing mental clarity. Make time for

regular physical activity to release pent-up stress and boost your mood.

- **Time Management:** Poor time management can lead to stress and burnout. Structure your day with prioritized tasks, and don't forget to make time for rest and relaxation.

Journaling as a Practice of Resiliency

Marcus Aurelius, one of the most famous Stoic philosophers, kept a personal journal called Meditations, in which he wrote about his struggles with anxiety, anger, and other negative emotions. By writing about his experiences, Aurelius was able to reflect on his thoughts and actions and gain a better understanding of himself. He also used his journal to remind himself of the Stoic principles he believed in, such as the impermanence of all things and the importance of living in accordance with nature.

Similarly, Epictetus, another famous Stoic philosopher, encouraged his students to keep a journal as a way of practicing self-reflection. He believed that by writing down our thoughts and experiences, we can better understand ourselves and our place in the world. This self-awareness can help us make better decisions and navigate difficult situations with more ease and resilience.

In modern times, the practice of journaling has become a popular tool for promoting self-reflection and personal growth. Many people use journaling as a way of processing their emotions and gaining clarity on their thoughts and experiences. By writing down our thoughts and feelings, we can gain a better understanding of ourselves and the world around us.

To practice stoicism through journaling, it can be helpful to begin by setting aside a few minutes each day to reflect on experiences and thoughts. This can be done in a physical journal, on a computer, or even on a smartphone app. Some key questions to consider during this reflection might include:

- What challenges did I face today?
- How did I respond to those challenges?
- Were my actions in line with my values?
- How can I apply the principles of stoicism to improve my response to future challenges?
- By regularly reflecting on these questions and others related to stoic philosophy, individuals can develop a more mindful and intentional approach to their daily lives. Over time, this practice can lead to greater resilience and a deeper sense of purpose.

To put Stoic philosophy into practice in our daily lives, we can start by incorporating some of the principles into our daily routines. For example, we can begin each day with a reflection on what is within our control and what is outside of our control. This can help us focus our energy on the things that we can change, rather than getting bogged down by the things that are beyond our influence.

We can also practice gratitude, which is a central tenet of Stoicism. By focusing on the things we are grateful for, we can shift our perspective and cultivate a more positive mindset. This can help us better cope with adversity and build resilience in the face of challenging circumstances.

Another way to put Stoic philosophy into practice is by embracing the concept of memento mori, which is Latin for "remember that you will die." This may sound morbid, but it is actually a way of reminding ourselves of the impermanence of all things and the importance of living each day to the fullest. By embracing the reality of our mortality, we can gain a greater appreciation for life and find meaning in the present moment.

One modern book that is particularly useful for anyone interested in practicing stoicism and learning more on the topic is "The Daily Stoic" by Ryan Holiday. This book provides a year's worth of daily meditations based on the teachings of the ancient stoic philosophers. Each day's meditation includes a short passage from the writings of a stoic philosopher, along with an interpretation and reflection from the author.

Other useful books for further study of stoicism include "Meditations" by Marcus Aurelius, "Letters from a Stoic" by Seneca, and "The Enchiridion" by Epictetus. These works provide a deeper understanding of the principles of stoicism and how they can be applied to everyday life.

Stoicism in Relationships

In intimate relationships, stoicism can help us navigate the ups and downs of our emotional lives. The stoic philosopher Epictetus advised that we should not let our emotions control us, but rather we should control our emotions. This does not mean suppressing our emotions, but rather recognizing that our emotions are under our control and can be managed through mindfulness and self-awareness. This can help us avoid the pitfalls of emotional reactivity, which can damage our relationships and our mental health.

In familial relationships, stoicism can help us navigate the challenges of family dynamics. The stoic philosopher Seneca wrote extensively on the importance of forgiveness and compassion in family relationships. He recognized that families are often sources of conflict and stress, but he also believed that we have a duty to love and care for our families, even in difficult circumstances. By practicing forgiveness and compassion, we can avoid holding grudges and resentments that can poison our relationships and erode our mental health.

In work relationships, stoicism can help us navigate the challenges of a competitive and stressful work environment. The stoic philosopher Marcus Aurelius believed that our work should be aligned with our values and that we should approach our work with a sense of purpose and meaning. This can help us stay focused on the things that matter most and avoid getting caught up in the petty dramas and politics of the workplace. By approaching our work with a stoic mindset, we can also avoid burnout and maintain a healthy work-life balance.

Tim Ferriss – Managing Stress and Decision Fatigue

Tim Ferriss, entrepreneur, investor, and author of *The 4-Hour Workweek*, has openly discussed his reliance on Stoic philosophy to manage stress and make better decisions. During challenging times in his career, Ferriss adopted key Stoic practices to overcome anxiety and achieve clarity.

- **Negative Visualization:** Ferriss uses this Stoic exercise to prepare for worst-case scenarios. By visualizing the potential loss of his career or investments, he not only reduces fear but also identifies practical solutions to minimize risks.
- **Emotional Mastery:** Ferriss applies the principle of emotional discipline to prevent knee-jerk reactions to stress. By practicing mindfulness and reflection, he

maintains focus on rational decision-making, even in high-pressure situations.
- **Simplifying Decisions:** Ferriss often employs the Stoic principle of focusing on essentials. He cuts out distractions and prioritizes tasks that align with his values and long-term goals, reducing mental fatigue.

Jeff Bezos – Focusing on Long-Term Thinking

Jeff Bezos, the founder of Amazon, unknowingly reflects Stoic principles through his focus on long-term thinking and emotional discipline. Bezos consistently emphasizes making decisions based on factors within his control and maintaining a forward-looking perspective.

- **Focus on Controllables:** Bezos often says, "Focus on the inputs, and the outputs will take care of themselves." By dedicating his energy to processes (what Amazon can control, like customer experience and innovation), he reduces stress over uncontrollable outcomes such as market competition.
- **Adversity as a Teacher:** In Amazon's early days, Bezos faced repeated setbacks, from funding challenges to technological failures. Instead of becoming discouraged, he viewed each obstacle as an opportunity to learn and improve the business.
- **Maintaining Perspective:** Bezos frequently reminds his team to focus on the bigger picture. By adopting a long-term mindset, he navigates short-term challenges without emotional overreaction.

Exercise for Founders: Building Your Stoic Resilience Plan

This exercise will help you integrate Stoic principles into your daily life and business to cultivate mental resilience and emotional mastery.

1. **The Dichotomy of Control List:**

- Write down two columns: "What I Can Control" and "What I Cannot Control." Include current challenges in your business.
- Focus your energy only on the items in the "What I Can Control" column.

2. **Daily Reflection:**

- Set aside 10 minutes at the end of each day to reflect on three key areas:
    - **What went well today?**
    - **What challenges did I face, and how did I respond?**
    - **What can I improve tomorrow?**

3. **Negative Visualization:**

- Spend 5 minutes imagining a worst-case scenario in your business (e.g., losing a major client or running out of funding).
- Write down actionable steps you would take to mitigate the risk or rebuild. This exercise reduces fear and boosts preparedness.

4. **Gratitude Practice:**

- Each morning, write down three things you are grateful for in your business and personal life.
- This simple habit helps shift your mindset to focus on abundance rather than scarcity.

5. **Develop a Resilience Mantra:**

- Create a personal mantra inspired by Stoic teachings (e.g., "Focus on the process, not the outcome" or "Adversity is my teacher").
- Repeat it whenever you face setbacks to reinforce a positive, resilient mindset.
- Our Mantra as a company & really a way we choose to lead our lives is "Own Your Purpose"

Develop Your Resilience Mantra

What is one mantra I can make today that will reinforce a positive & resilient mindset?

- _____

CHAPTER 4
FOUNDATIONAL HEALTH FOR FOUNDERS

Your Brain on Food: How Your Diet Influences Decision-Making and Leadership

Ever find yourself staring at your screen at 3 p.m., unable to make a simple decision like choosing between two nearly identical fonts? You start questioning life choices: Should you have pursued interpretive dance instead of entrepreneurship? If this sounds familiar, your lunch might be the real culprit, not your career path.

Your role as a founder demands making countless decisions each day, from high-stakes strategic moves to deciding if it's appropriate to add emojis to investor emails (hint: probably not). Surprisingly, your ability to make these crucial decisions isn't solely a product of your business acumen or charisma—it also hinges heavily on what's on your plate.

Why Food Matters More Than Your MBA (Sort of)

Think of your brain as the ultimate control room for your startup empire. It manages critical thinking, problem-solving, stress responses, and your ability to inspire a team—even the slightly passive-aggressive guy in IT. Feeding your brain premium fuel is non-negotiable if you want to perform at peak levels. Let's break down how food acts as the "medicine" that either boosts or busts your leadership game.

Blood Sugar Rollercoasters: Fun at the Fair, Not in the Boardroom

When your blood sugar spikes after devouring a donut (or five—no judgment), it feels great...for about ten minutes. Then the inevitable crash hits. This cycle of spikes and dips isn't just annoying; it significantly impairs your ability to concentrate, maintain a balanced mood, and avoid snapping at your intern for forgetting your coffee (again). Opting instead for whole foods rich in healthy fats and proteins creates steady energy, letting you tackle tasks without plotting a nap beneath your desk.

Neurotransmitters: Chemical Messengers You Should Actually Listen To

Dopamine and serotonin aren't just cool words for cocktail parties—they're neurotransmitters directly influenced by your diet. Foods rich in omega-3 fatty acids (think salmon, walnuts, chia seeds) and quality proteins boost these critical brain chemicals, enhancing your mood, motivation, and overall cognitive clarity. Conversely, a diet filled with processed foods is like sending spam emails to your neurotransmitters—confusing, annoying, and eventually causing your brain to click 'unsubscribe.'

Your Gut: The CEO of Your Mood and Mind

Did you know your gut is home to trillions of bacteria working diligently to influence your brain's functioning? Yep, there's an entire ecosystem in your digestive tract whispering messages to your mind. This "gut-brain axis" directly impacts your decision-making abilities, stress responses, and overall mental health. Eating fiber-rich foods (veggies, legumes, whole grains) and fermented options like sauerkraut and kombucha promotes a harmonious gut environment. Ignore this, and you're essentially hosting a hostile takeover in your own gut, complete with digestive discomfort, anxiety, and brain fog.

Inflammation: The Silent Killer of Good Ideas

Chronic inflammation is the business world's equivalent of the endless PowerPoint presentation—exhausting, detrimental to your mental clarity, and impossible to ignore. Inflammation isn't just about swollen ankles; it's oxidative stress that damages your cells, DNA, and cognitive function. Constant stress (hello, entrepreneurship) fuels inflammation, leading to impaired judgment, emotional instability, and decreased productivity. Combat this by incorporating anti-inflammatory superstars like leafy greens, berries, fatty fish, turmeric, and nuts into your meals. Think of these foods as strategic consultants hired to streamline your body's operations and cut down on inflammatory inefficiencies.

Crafting a Nutrition Plan That Won't Make You Cry Into Your Salad

Let's be real: founders are busy. Grabbing whatever food is within arm's reach (typically leftover pizza from last night's "strategy session") often feels like the only viable option. But thoughtful planning can dramatically enhance your daily performance:

1. Prioritize Whole Foods: Fresh veggies, lean proteins, whole grains, and healthy fats stabilize energy and mood, turning your afternoon slump into a productivity power hour.
2. Plan Ahead: Meal prep isn't just for Instagram influencers. Even basic planning—like keeping healthy snacks in your office—can prevent desperate vending machine visits.
3. Balance Your Macronutrients: Pairing proteins and healthy fats with fiber-rich carbs prevents energy crashes. Think avocado and eggs on whole-grain toast, not a double espresso and pastry.
4. Omega-3 Power: Regularly consuming omega-3 fatty acids from fish, walnuts, or flaxseeds is like regularly updating your brain's software—everything just runs smoother.
5. Hydration Station: Water isn't just necessary for survival; it's critical for optimal cognitive function. If you're thirsty, you're already behind the hydration curve.
6. Mind Your Caffeine and Sugar: Coffee is sacred, we know. But relying heavily on caffeine and sugar sets you up for mood swings and anxiety spikes. Choose steady nourishment over momentary jolts.

Restoring Balance: Becoming a Zen Master of Health

Restoring health isn't just about diet; it's a holistic strategy involving physical activity, mindfulness, and connecting with nature. Gardening, hiking, or supporting local agriculture doesn't just enhance your Instagram feed—it actually fosters a profound biological reconnection, reducing stress and inflammation. Consider these activities mandatory team-building exercises for you and your trillions of gut bacteria friends.

Final Thoughts: You Are What You Eat, Literally

In short, if you're serious about leadership, you can't ignore your diet. Eating intentionally isn't merely a luxury—it's a foundational investment in your cognitive capabilities and emotional resilience. By choosing foods that heal rather than harm, you're proactively steering your body away from inflammation and toward optimal functioning. After all, your brain is your most precious startup resource—feed it wisely, and it'll take you to heights even interpretive dance couldn't rival.

Optimize Your Body. Expand Your Capacity. Build Resilience.

In a world that demands relentless drive from leaders, visionaries, and entrepreneurs, your health is your foundational asset. It's not just about energy or focus—it's about sustainability. If your body breaks down, your mission will too. This chapter is your tactical guide to reclaiming physical resilience by focusing on the highest-leverage habits: gut health, detoxing your kitchen, mastering nutrient-dense meals, and optimizing your metabolism through intermittent fasting and smart supplementation.

We're not here to drown you in theory. We're here to equip you with proven tools and protocols that will immediately impact how you feel, perform, and lead.

Gut Check: What's Growing in Your Gut Is Growing in Your Life

Many founders unknowingly battle chronic fatigue, brain fog, anxiety, or inflammation because of gut imbalances—specifically, **candida overgrowth**. Candida is a yeast that naturally exists in your body but can proliferate rapidly when fed by a diet high in processed carbs, sugars, alcohol, and stress. Left unchecked, it disrupts digestion, weakens immunity, and sabotages mental clarity.

The Anti-Candida Protocol (Yeast Cleanse)

Step-by-step:

1. **Purchase**: 1 container each of organic raspberries and blackberries + Saccharomyces Boulardii capsules.
2. **Blend the berries** into a purée.
3. **Mix in** the contents of one capsule of S. Boulardii.
4. **Cover loosely** with a paper towel or plastic wrap—do not seal airtight.
5. **Ferment** in a cool dark space for 3 days, stirring once daily.
6. **Consume 1 tbsp daily** on an empty stomach until gone.
7. **Avoid sugar, processed carbs, and alcohol** during this protocol.

This approach introduces a **"sacrificial yeast"** that outcompetes the candida for food, eventually starving it out and allowing your gut to reset. Expect improvements in digestion, clarity, and even skin health.

Detox Your Kitchen, Detox Your Life

If it's in your house, you're going to eat it. Willpower is not enough when you're sleep-deprived or stressed. You need an environment that supports your intentions, not one that sabotages them.

Your Kitchen Detox Checklist:

Toss anything that falls under these categories:

- Ultra-processed carbs (white bread, crackers, cereal, flour)
- Sugary snacks, juices, and sodas
- Cow's milk and most cheeses (high in inflammatory casomorphins)
- Anything with vegetable oils or hydrogenated fats
- Old canned goods or anything packaged with BPA linings
- Condiments with added sugar or inflammatory oils

Pro Tip: Do this with a friend or partner to hold you accountable. Involve your kids. Explain the "why." Empower them to choose health with you.

Still have family members who aren't on board?

Designate separate shelves—yours for nutrient-dense foods, theirs for compromise items. Out of sight = out of mind.

Set Up Your Pantry for Success

A stocked pantry is like a well-funded startup—it gives you leverage. When healthy meals are simple and flavorful, you're more likely to stay consistent. This is where the **WITF Cooking Theory** comes in: *Whatever's In The Fridge*.

You don't need a fancy recipe. You just need a solid pantry of healthy staples + a few fresh ingredients, and you can whip up Thai, Greek, Indian, or Latin-inspired meals in minutes.

Base Categories:

- **Fats**: Olive oil, ghee, coconut oil, sesame oil

- **Acids**: Vinegars (balsamic, rice, red wine), lemon, lime
- **Spices/Herbs**: Cumin, turmeric, oregano, garlic, paprika, ginger, thyme, cilantro
- **Vegetables**: Sweet potato, cucumber, spinach, mushrooms, tomato, bell pepper, eggplant
- **Proteins**: Chicken, lamb, fish, garbanzo beans, goat cheese, eggs

Build your pantry slowly. Each grocery trip, grab one or two items per category until you've got a full culinary toolkit.

Want Greek tonight? Olive oil + oregano + lemon + dill + feta = done.

Feeling Indian? Ghee + turmeric + cumin + garam masala + chickpeas = you're there.

Craving Latin flavors? Coconut oil + chili powder + garlic + avocado + lime—easy.

Let cooking be creative, not constrictive. With the WITF approach, healthy eating becomes effortless and fun.

Nutrient Density, Macros & Meal Building

You don't have to count every gram of food—but it helps to **understand how to fuel with intention**. Focus on building every plate around protein, fiber, healthy fats, and colorful vegetables.

Macro Basics:

- **Protein**: 0.5–1.25g per lb of body weight depending on goals
- **Carbs**: 0.5–1.5g per lb depending on activity level

- **Fats**: Fill in the remainder of your daily calories

Use this formula to calculate your starting macros: **Body weight (lbs) x 15 = estimated daily calorie needs**

Then break that down into grams of protein, carbs, and fat using the formulas provided earlier.

Pro Tip: Divide your daily target by how many meals you eat to make meal prep effortless.

Intermittent Fasting and Autophagy: The Founder's Advantage

Fasting isn't about deprivation—it's about strategy. It stimulates **autophagy**, your body's natural process of cleaning out damaged cells and making room for regeneration. Combine this with nutrient-dense eating and you'll unlock better energy, reduced inflammation, and enhanced focus.

Getting Started with Intermittent Fasting:

- **Start with 12:12** (12 hours fasting, 12 eating)
- Gradually work up to **16:8**
- Prioritize hydration, electrolytes, and whole foods when breaking your fast
- **Avoid sugar or alcohol**—both disrupt gut and hormonal function

Once fat-adapted, your body becomes metabolically flexible—burning carbs when available and switching to fats when fasting.

Closing Thoughts: Physical Resilience Fuels Purpose

You're not just a founder—you're a system. And if one system breaks down, the rest follows. By anchoring your lifestyle in nutrient-dense food, smart fasting, kitchen mastery, and gut health, you create a physiological foundation strong enough to carry your mission.

Start simple. Clean your kitchen. Build your pantry. Follow the yeast protocol. Try WITF cooking once this week. These aren't chores—they're stepping stones to long-term clarity, stamina, and impact.

CHAPTER 5
MASTERING EMOTIONAL AND SPIRITUAL INTELLIGENCE

Owning Your Purpose and Connecting It to Your Business

One of the most transformative elements of successful leadership is clarity of purpose. As a founder, your sense of purpose is the North Star that guides you through the highs and lows of entrepreneurship. It fuels your passion, drives your actions, and shapes your company's culture. But finding and truly owning your purpose isn't always easy. It requires introspection, vulnerability, and a deep understanding of your values, beliefs, and what you stand for.

Purpose-driven leadership is at the core of what makes a successful founder. When your personal mission aligns with the mission of your company, it creates a powerful synergy that resonates not only with your team but also with customers, partners, and investors. This alignment is what fuels long-term success, especially in the face of challenges and adversity.

How to Discover Your Purpose

- Reflect on Your Values: Begin by identifying your core values. What do you stand for? What principles guide your actions? These values are the building blocks of your purpose and should inform every decision you make in your business.

- Identify Your 'Why': Ask yourself why you started your business in the first place. Was it to solve a problem? Create something innovative? Serve a community? Your 'why' should be more than just financial success. It should be about creating a meaningful impact.

- Align Your Business with Your Purpose: Once you've identified your purpose, make sure it's embedded in every aspect of your business, from your product or service to your company culture and values. When your company's mission aligns with your personal values, your leadership becomes more authentic and compelling.

Owning your purpose creates clarity, focus, and a sense of fulfillment. It allows you to lead with authenticity, and inspire your team to follow your vision. When purpose is clear, every decision becomes easier because it's aligned with your deeper mission.

The Importance of Meditation and Mental Hygiene

Emotional intelligence — the ability to understand and manage your emotions and the emotions of others — is one of the most important leadership skills a founder can develop. However, emotional intelligence doesn't just come naturally; it requires consistent practice and reflection. One of the most effective ways to cultivate emotional intelligence is through meditation and mental hygiene.

Just as you take care of your physical health, it's equally important to maintain mental hygiene. Your mind is constantly processing information, emotions, and experiences, and if it's not properly cleaned and nurtured, it can become cluttered, overwhelmed, and stressed. Meditation helps you clear the mental clutter, improve emotional regulation, and deepen your self-awareness.

The Power of Meditation for Founders

- Stress Reduction: Meditation has been shown to reduce stress and anxiety, which are common among founders. By calming the mind and focusing on the present moment, meditation helps you manage stress more effectively.

- Improved Focus and Clarity: Through regular meditation, you train your mind to focus, which enhances your ability to make clear, thoughtful decisions. When you clear your mental space, you can see your business challenges from a new perspective and come up with creative solutions.

- Emotional Regulation: As a founder, you'll face many emotional highs and lows. Meditation teaches you to observe your emotions without becoming overwhelmed by them, which improves emotional intelligence and helps you lead with greater composure and empathy.

Simple Meditation Practices for Founders

- Mindful Breathing: Start your day by sitting quietly and focusing on your breath. Take deep, slow breaths, and bring your attention to the sensation of air moving in and out of your body. This practice calms the nervous system and centers your mind.

- Body Scan: This meditation technique involves focusing on each part of your body, from head to toe, noticing any tension or discomfort. It's a great way to release physical and emotional stress, especially after a long, demanding day.
- Gratitude Meditation: Spend a few minutes focusing on things you're grateful for, whether it's your health, your team, or the progress your business has made. Gratitude meditation helps shift your mindset from scarcity to abundance, improving both mental clarity and emotional well-being.

By incorporating meditation and mental hygiene into your routine, you'll increase your emotional intelligence, reduce stress, and improve your decision-making. As you develop a calm, focused, and centered mind, you'll be better equipped to lead with authenticity and compassion.

Healing from Past Traumas to Unlock Your Full Potential

Every founder has a story, and many of those stories come with personal challenges and emotional wounds. Whether it's past failures, family dynamics, or personal insecurities, these unresolved issues can manifest in your business decisions, leadership style, and relationships.

Healing from past traumas is not a process that happens overnight, but it is essential for unlocking your full potential as a leader. When you carry emotional baggage, it can cloud your judgment, trigger stress responses, and hinder your ability to connect with others. By addressing and healing from these traumas, you free yourself to be the best version of yourself in your personal and professional life.

How Unresolved Trauma Affects Your Leadership

- Decision-Making: Unresolved emotional issues can lead to decision fatigue or clouded judgment. You may make choices based on fear or insecurity, rather than rational thinking or strategic planning.
- Relationship Struggles: Past traumas can affect how you interact with your team, partners, and clients. You may find yourself reacting defensively or withdrawing emotionally when faced with challenges, which can undermine trust and collaboration.
- Emotional Overload: Founders are often under a great deal of stress, and unresolved trauma can amplify these feelings, making it harder to manage your emotions in a healthy way.

Steps Toward Healing

- Seek Professional Support: Therapy, counseling, or coaching can provide a safe space to explore and heal from past trauma. A professional can guide you through the process of self-discovery, helping you release emotional blockages and gain insight into your behavior.
- Forgive Yourself: Self-compassion is an essential part of healing. Recognize that everyone makes mistakes, and that your past does not define your future. By forgiving yourself, you can create space for personal growth and unlock your potential as a leader.
- Practice Emotional Release: Activities such as journaling, art, or physical exercise can help you release pent-up emotions. These outlets allow you to process and express your feelings, which can facilitate healing and emotional clarity.

Healing from past traumas is a deeply personal journey, but it's a crucial step toward becoming a resilient, emotionally intelligent founder. As you heal, you'll gain the emotional freedom and clarity needed to lead with purpose and authenticity.

Embracing Vulnerability and Fostering Meaningful Connections

True leadership requires vulnerability. As a founder, it's easy to feel like you have to project an image of strength and certainty at all times. But vulnerability — the willingness to show up as your authentic self, flaws and all — is what truly connects you with others and inspires trust.

Leaders who embrace vulnerability create an environment where people feel safe to express their ideas, take risks, and contribute fully to the team's success. Vulnerability fosters deep, meaningful connections and helps cultivate a culture of empathy and collaboration.

Why Vulnerability is Key to Effective Leadership

- Builds Trust: When you show vulnerability, you model openness and honesty. This encourages your team to do the same, creating an atmosphere of mutual trust and respect.

- Encourages Innovation: A culture that embraces vulnerability allows people to express ideas without fear of judgment. This leads to greater creativity and innovation, as everyone feels empowered to contribute.

- Fosters Authentic Relationships: Vulnerability helps you connect with your team and stakeholders on a deeper level. When people feel seen, heard, and understood, they are more likely to invest in your vision and support your mission.

How to Embrace Vulnerability as a Founder

- Share Your Struggles: Don't be afraid to share the challenges you're facing. Be transparent about your mistakes and the lessons you've learned. This authenticity will resonate with your team and show them that growth comes from overcoming obstacles.
- Ask for Help: As a founder, it can be tempting to try to do everything on your own. But asking for help — whether from mentors, peers, or your team — shows strength, not weakness. It fosters a culture of collaboration and shared responsibility.
- Be Open to Feedback: Invite feedback from your team and be open to constructive criticism. Vulnerability means being willing to listen to others and grow from their insights.

By embracing vulnerability, you'll not only become a more emotionally intelligent leader, but you'll also create a more resilient, connected team. Vulnerability is the gateway to authentic leadership and lasting success.

Owning Your Purpose

What do we mean by Own Your Purpose?

It is one thing to identify one's purpose in life, which is no petty task for most, but to take ownership of that revelation requires significant strength and courage to overcome the many hurdles that consciously and sometimes subconsciously prevent us from ever progressing towards the fulfilling life that was meant for us. In this segment, I will break down the psychological construct of what it means to have "purpose" in life, how to identify what our purpose is, the roadblocks likely preventing you from finding it in the first place and finish with a discussion on how to work towards taking ownership of our purpose in life.

> "Happiness is the meaning and purpose of life, the whole aim and end of human existence."
> **– Gretchen Rubin, The Happiness Project**

What are your core values?

Before we begin the discussion on identifying our purpose in life, it is important that we get clear on what it means to us to be authentic. It is important to choose goals or live in a way that resonates with your authentic values. According to Sonja Lyubomirsky in "The How of Happiness," having "authentic goals" is **crucial** for dedicated goal pursuit. **The goals we set should be intrinsically enjoyable or meaningful**. While specific tasks within a larger pursuit, such as individual courses and exams in medical school, may not bring immediate joy, the overarching goal of contributing to the well-being of others can be deeply fulfilling. Pursuing outcomes that align with genuine values serves as a motivating force, enabling individuals to persist even in the face of obstacles, set backs, failures and tedium.

Why does embracing authenticity contribute to happiness?

At its core, authenticity creates an environment where we can engage in activities and connect with people we genuinely love, and steer clear of those that don't resonate with us. Authenticity is an expression of vulnerability and grants us the freedom to respond in ways that feel genuine and comfortable.

Delving into psychological theory provides additional insights into why authenticity is linked to increased happiness.

- First, it reduces **cognitive dissonance**, a psychological discomfort arising from inconsistencies in our actions and statements. Authenticity aligns our words and deeds with our values, minimizing the likelihood of experiencing this discomfort.
- Second, embracing authenticity moves us towards **intrinsic motivation**, making goals that align with our true selves more likely to be personally identified or fully integrated. When the outcome of a behavior resonates with our values, our motivation to sustain that behavior is enhanced.
- Lastly, authenticity helps preserve **willpower**. Acting in ways that feel unnatural depletes our willpower, potentially leading to indulgence in unhealthy or goal-inconsistent behaviors. Being true to ourselves safeguards our willpower for use in confronting more challenging situations.

Core values guide your behaviors, decisions and actions. When living, working or behaving in alignment with your core values life will seem much more fulfilling and bring about a sense of purpose, clarity and self awareness. By taking the time to identify your core values, you can ensure that any decision you make is in line with what's important to you and the type of person you want to be. It is not uncommon for us to have what we would consider a core value and not be living in alignment with it. It is also normal for our values to change over time, at different points in your career, in relationships you maintain, when it comes to decisions we make regarding our health, or finances. Things that are important to us change over time and so will our values.

Identify 5 core values

Identifying your core values is a vital step in setting an intention to discover your life purpose. These values serve as guiding principles for your behaviors, decisions, and actions. Living in alignment with what truly matters to you fosters a sense of greater fulfillment, clarity, and self-awareness, ultimately paving the way to a more purposeful life. Below is a list of values compiled by Brene Brown, lead researcher into shame, guilt and vulnerability. Choose 5 from this list or you can write your own.

Accountability	Calmness	Contribution
Accuracy	Challenge	Control
Achievement	Cheerfulness	Cooperation
Action	Citizenship	Courage`
Adventure	Clarity	Courtesy
Altruism	Commitment	Creativity
Ambition	Common Sense	Curiosity
Assertiveness	Community	Decisiveness
Authenticity	Compassion	Democracy
Authority	Competency	Dependability
Autonomy	Competition	Determination
Balance	Consistency	Diligence
Beauty	Contentment	Discipline
Belonging	Continuous Improvement	Discretion
Boldness		Diversity

Effectiveness	Friendship	Joy
Efficiency	Fun	Justice
Elegance	Generosity	Kindness
Empathy	Grace	Knowledge
Enjoyment	Growth	Leadership
Enthusiasm	Happiness	Learning
Equality	Hard Work	Legacy
Equity	Harmony	Love
Excellence	Health	Loyalty
Excitement	Helping	Mastery
Expertise	Holiness	Meaning
Exploration	Honesty	Obedience
Fairness	Honor	Openness
Faith	Humility	Optimism
Fame	Humor	Order
Family	Independence	Originality
Fidelity	Influence	
Fitness	Ingenuity	Peace
Flexibility	Inquisitiveness	Perfection
Fluency	Insight	Pleasure
Focus	Intelligence	Poise
Freedom	Intuition	Positivity

Practicality	Self-control	Support
Preparedness	Selflessness	Teamwork
Professionalism	Self-reliance	Temperance
Prudence	Sensitivity	Thoroughness
Quality	Serenity	Thoughtfulness
Recognition	Service	Timeliness
Reliability	Simplicity	Tolerance
Religion	Soundness	Trustworthiness
Reputation	Speed	Truth
Resourcefulness	Spirituality	Understanding
Respect	Spontaneity	Uniqueness
Responsibility	Stability	Unity
Restraint	Strategic	Vision
Security	Strength	Vitality
Self-actualization	Structure	Wealth
	Success	Wisdom

These will be your guidelines when looking to identify your purpose in life.

Write your 5 core values in order of importance.

1. _____
2. _____
3. _____
4. _____

5. _____

What do these values say about you?

Why are these important to you?

Why did you select #1 as the most important?

What is Purpose?

While definitions of purpose have varied in the past, more recently a consensus has emerged: a purpose in life represents a stable and generalized intention to accomplish something that is at once personally meaningful and at the same time leads to productive engagement with some aspect of the world beyond the self (Damon, Menon, & Bronk, 2003). This definition includes at least three important components, including a goal orientation, personal meaningfulness, and a focus on aims beyond the self. (John Templeton Foundation, The Psychology of Purpose, 2018)

Two things that keep you from finding your purpose:

Comfortability and fear of change

Whether we care to admit it or not, change is hard. One of the best analogies I have heard on the subject is to imagine that we are affixed to a pole with a large rubber band where the pole represents our current state; our decent paying job, decent relationship, decent home, or our current health situation for example. The rubber band representing the overwhelming resistance we have to change, as whenever we entertain the idea of or try to do something different than what we are doing already, like end a relationship that we know is not in our best interest, or quit our job and start a business doing something we love, the rubber band snaps us back to our baseline, where we feel safe and comfortable, where action isn't really required to maintain our status quo. Where we can avoid putting ourselves at risk of failure and disappointment. Therefore, in order to avoid the seemingly inevitable situation of cognitive dissonance, leading us to justify our lack of success, we stay put. Clearly this is a problem if your goal is to become healthier or to leave the monotonous and unfulfilling conditions we are currently in and step into our purpose in a way that provides us with a sense of meaning in our lives.

Limiting Beliefs

Limiting beliefs are nothing more than the story we tell ourselves about who we are and what we are capable of leading to a life of mediocrity, self sabotage and frankly unrealized potential.

In order to move past our limiting beliefs, largely developed in childhood, we need to familiarize ourselves with this belief system and the story we tell ourselves about who we are and what we are capable of. Our beliefs, both good or bad, carry with them strong emotions which are the major drivers behind our actions.

Step 1: Identify any negative beliefs that you have involving each of the 4 domains of resilience, **health, economics, relationships and opportunities**. Once you have listed out each negative or limiting belief, begin by asking yourself if it is true or not. What are you telling yourself that you can or can't do about each of these domains of your life?

Step 2: Turn any negative belief you identified into a positive and empowering belief. The only limitations we have are the ones we create for ourselves. By reframing these negative or limiting beliefs, you will likely find that they are a by-product of a lack of certainty, not in line with your values and simply an excuse to keep you comfortable where you're at.

*If you are struggling with step 2 try taking this [Strengths Assessment](#) and looking back to the core values you selected to give you a good place to start.

Ownership

The Concept of Personal Accountability:

Truly embracing the idea of being personally accountable for one's actions, to include the fulfillment of one's destiny can be quite challenging for most as our culture and society at large have made it seem like external forces are a much larger determinant of how our lives play out and what we are capable of. When we acknowledge that we are the architects of our own lives and free to choose how to act, behave, and feel, the idea of external limitations begins to fall away, allowing us to abandon the "victim mindset".

"I would like to share a story to help illustrate this point. I remember vividly, as a college student after serving 8 years active duty in the military hearing some fellow students complain about the language barrier having a foreign graduate assistant leading labs in one of our biology courses, and being worried about failing because of it. At the time I found it humorous that so many of my classmates were so hyper-focused on this because everything that we needed to learn was in our textbook, and I personally could care less about the grad assistants lectures because in many of them I felt I had a better grasp on the topic then they did. All I was doing was reading my text book, taking notes in class and if needed, searching the internet for more contextual information regarding the subject either in the form of youtube videos or science journals. The difference between myself and those other students who were complaining is that I hadn't considered that I needed someone else to teach me the information and took responsibility for my education and became an active participant in the learning process. This, mind you, is what most professionals do in their respective fields.

You may be thinking that this mindset is one that was developed over time from my years in service, and to some extent I would say you are probably right, but there was a defining moment for me actually during my last year of service where I had come to the realization that I had been merely regurgitating or emulating what I had heard or witnessed from others. Disgusted with myself, I made a very conscious decision to no longer be that kind of a person. To me, it started with believing in myself in a sort of blind, child-like faith manner which resulted in me realizing that that blind faith wasn't unwarranted. I discovered that I can literally do whatever I want in a way that I previously hadn't realized.

As you can imagine this only emblazoned my resolve to embrace personal accountability as I witnessed the results time and time again. I went from what most would refer to as a below average student who barely graduated high school to being referred to as a genius by literally all of my friends and family. The only thing that changed was that I began to take full responsibility for myself and let go of deterministic ideas about who I was and what I was capable of achieving." - James Artman

Most scientists are aware of the phenomenon of the unconditioned mind, exemplified notably in the field of genetics. In 1913, at Columbia University, 19-year-old freshman Alfred Henry Sturtevant made a groundbreaking discovery that fundamentally shaped the understanding of genetics.

Working under the guidance of Thomas Hunt Morgan and drawing upon a decade's worth of research, Sturtevant realized he could map genes' positions on chromosomes by observing their inheritance patterns in fruit flies. His innovative approach provided geneticists with a revolutionary tool, laying the groundwork for modern genetic mapping techniques and securing his legacy as a pioneer in genetics.

Had Sturtevant allowed himself to be constrained by societal conditioning—believing he was too young or inexperienced to achieve such insights—he might never have made this transformative discovery. Such breakthroughs are accessible to anyone willing to embrace personal accountability and challenge their perceived limitations.

Life Happens for You

Adopting the perspective that life happens for you, rather than to you, significantly enhances the ability to identify and own one's purpose. This mindset views challenges, setbacks, and experiences as opportunities for growth and learning, rather than as obstacles. Believing that life's events occur for one's benefit fosters introspection and active participation in one's personal narrative, turning challenges into stepping stones and failures into valuable lessons.

This outlook cultivates resilience and perseverance, empowering individuals to remain committed to their paths, recognizing each experience as integral to uncovering their unique purpose. Rather than ruminating on setbacks, reframing negative self-talk and obstacles into positive and constructive perspectives becomes pivotal.

Strategies to Shift Mindset

Practice Self-Awareness

- **Recognize Negative Thoughts**: Identify instances of negative self-talk.
- **Monitor Emotions**: Notice emotional responses and consciously choose how to respond.

Challenge Negative Thoughts

- **Question Assumptions**: Evaluate the accuracy of negative thoughts.
- **Consider Alternative Perspectives**: Adopt balanced interpretations of situations.

Cognitive Reappraisal

- **Replace Negative Thoughts**: Substitute negative thoughts with affirming, realistic statements. As Elizabeth Bernstein states in the Wall Street Journal, cognitive reappraisal involves reframing thoughts constructively, grounded in reality.
- **Focus on Strengths**: Emphasize personal strengths and past successes to build confidence.

As Byron Katie notes, "Life is simple. Everything happens for you, not to you. Everything happens at exactly the right moment, neither too soon nor too late. You don't have to like it—it's just easier if you do."

Focus on Abundance

Gratitude

Gratitude consistently ranks at the top of strategies for personal growth. Being consciously aware of one's blessings through optimism maintains humility, positivity, and appreciation, especially during challenging times. Gratitude propels individuals toward action rather than negativity, boosting motivation, energy, focus, and hope for the future. Incorporating daily gratitude practices, such as listing blessings each morning, significantly enhances overall well-being.

Resourcefulness

Operating from scarcity induces fight, flight, or freeze responses, severely limiting problem-solving capabilities. Persistent focus on deficits fosters a perpetual sense of inadequacy, hindering future planning and decision-making. This scarcity mindset reinforces self-defeating actions, perpetuating negative cycles. Shifting toward abundance, as highlighted by Shafir (2013) in "Scarcity: Why Having Too Little Means So Much," frees mental bandwidth, enabling constructive problem-solving and clearer decision-making.

The Parable of Green Pastures (Psalm 23)

"He makes me lie down in green pastures; He leads me beside the still waters." (Psalm 23:2)

Bible historian Ray Vander Laan illustrates that the "green pastures" described in Psalm 23 were never lush fields but sparse, scattered tufts of grass—enough to sustain sheep day by day. This allegory effectively conveys the principle of sufficiency, reassuring individuals that their needs will be met daily, thus mitigating anxiety about financial security.

Embracing this perspective allows mental clarity and the capacity to address challenges constructively rather than succumbing to anxiety-driven paralysis or self-destructive behaviors.

Identify What Brings Joy

Human brains are finely attuned to identifying sources of genuine pleasure beyond superficial hedonic impulses. Mindfulness about personal joys—such as the scent of fresh-cut grass or the invigorating chill of autumn—provides insight into activities aligned with one's values and purpose. Childhood and adult experiences often profoundly influence personal passion and purpose. Reflecting on positive and negative experiences, objects, and acts of service helps identify energizing and meaningful endeavors, fostering a purpose-driven life aligned with individual values.

CHAPTER 6
LIFE IS FULL OF CHOICES

Founder HERO: A Holistic Path to Purpose Driven Success

> *"The prescription for healing is within ourselves."*
> **— James Artman**

If there's one truth that every resilient founder must internalize, it's this: **resilience is a choice**. It's not reserved for the lucky or the genetically gifted. It's not some mystical force that only shows up during extreme hardship. It is a skill—a muscle—and it starts with a choice. A choice to take ownership. To lead yourself first. To tune into the inner voice of reason, courage, and hope instead of drowning in fear, excuses, or inertia.

Take Charge of Your Inner Dialogue

Healing, growth, transformation—they all begin from within. You already carry the wisdom, strength, and insight required to move forward. The challenge isn't finding the answers. It's trusting yourself enough to listen.

You have a voice inside that knows what to do next. It urges you to get up, try again, say no, set a boundary, forgive, or take that leap. The problem? That voice often gets muffled by fear, shame, trauma, or the comfort of complacency.

To become resilient, you must **amplify your proactive voice**. Choose to let it lead. Every time you act on its guidance, you reinforce your belief that you can navigate anything.

Emotional Mastery Is Spiritual Strength

Spiritual resilience isn't about perfection—it's about **presence**. It's not the absence of emotion, but the capacity to sit with those emotions without letting them hijack your decisions.

Life will test you. But in every moment of frustration, heartbreak, or stress, you are presented with a fork in the road: **reaction or response**. Reactivity is ego-driven. It lashes out, shuts down, or distracts. Response is grounded. It's the founder who pauses before the email, breathes before the argument, and chooses who they want to be instead of what the moment tries to dictate.

This is emotional regulation. And it's a non-negotiable for anyone who wants to lead with vision, integrity, and peace.

Everything Is a Choice

Even when it doesn't feel like it—**you are choosing.** Anger, jealousy, procrastination, avoidance—these aren't accidents. They're reactions rooted in old protective patterns. But once you see them, you have the power to shift them.

Every reaction is an opportunity to ask: *Is this my ego trying to protect itself? Or is this my higher self choosing peace, clarity, and alignment?* The more often you ask this, the more you return to the driver's seat of your life.

Believe in Yourself—Like a Kid Believes in Magic

When was the last time you approached life with the same faith as a child does—believing everything is possible?

Self-belief isn't something you wait to feel. It's something you **build through action**. Every time you try something new, finish what you start, or challenge yourself, you're casting a vote for the person you're becoming.

This forms a **self-worth feedback loop**: Challenge yourself → Achieve something new → Reinforce confidence → Repeat.

It's not about proving anything to the world. It's about proving to yourself that you can trust you. That you're capable. That you're resilient.

Try New Things—Stay Curious

Burnout doesn't always come from overwork. It often comes from undernourishment—spiritually, creatively, emotionally. Curiosity is the antidote.

Resilient founders stay curious. They ask better questions. They try unfamiliar foods, explore new hobbies, and lead with different perspectives. They're not obsessed with perfect outcomes—they're focused on **engagement with the process**.

When you focus on the journey, you reduce performance anxiety and keep your spirit alive and adaptable.

Take Radical Responsibility

At the core of spiritual resilience is **personal accountability**. The moment you stop outsourcing your problems—and your healing—to others is the moment you take back your power.

When you own your choices, your actions, and your results, everything changes:

- You become empowered to take action instead of waiting for change.
- You begin to reflect more deeply, gaining clarity on what drives you.
- You stop being the victim of circumstance and start becoming the architect of your future.

Personal accountability also means:

1. **Learning from your mistakes**, not being defined by them.
2. Acting in alignment with your **core values**, even when it's hard.
3. Building **trust and authenticity** in your relationships through follow-through.
4. **Breaking patterns** that no longer serve you.
5. Being **proactive** in solving problems instead of complaining about them.
6. Cultivating **humility and compassion** through the recognition of your imperfections.

The Founder's Power

Life is full of choices. Some small. Some seismic. But they all matter. Because together, they shape your identity, your impact, and your inner peace.

Resilience is not something you have or don't have. It's something you choose.

Choose to take charge. Choose to regulate. Choose to believe. Choose to explore. Choose to own it.

Because when you do, you become unstoppable—not because life gets easier, but because you've decided to meet it with your full self.

CHAPTER 7
CURATING YOUR ENVIRONMENT FOR SUCCESS

The Impact of Epigenetics and Environmental Factors

As a founder, you are often at the helm of decisions that affect both your personal well-being and your business. While your mindset, health, and emotional intelligence are essential for success, the environment around you plays an equally significant role in shaping your performance, creativity, and resilience.

Epigenetics, the study of how environmental factors affect gene expression, teaches us that our surroundings influence not just our immediate well-being but also our long-term potential. Everything from the physical space in which you work, the people you interact with, to the energy and atmosphere you cultivate can either enhance or hinder your performance.

Understanding the profound impact of environmental factors is critical for founders who want to operate at their highest potential. By curating an environment that fosters productivity, clarity, and focus, you set the stage for both personal and business growth.

How Your Environment Shapes Your Success

- Cognitive Function: Studies show that cluttered, chaotic environments can hinder cognitive function, increase stress levels, and reduce focus. On the other hand, a well-organized and calming space promotes mental clarity, creativity, and decision-making abilities.
- Emotional State: The people you interact with daily can significantly influence your emotional state. Positive, supportive relationships can elevate your mood, while toxic interactions or negative energy can drain your motivation and morale.
- Productivity and Flow: Your work environment directly impacts your ability to enter flow states—those moments when you're fully immersed in a task and performing at your highest level. A cluttered or distracting environment can impede your ability to reach this state, while a purposefully designed environment can enhance it.

To be the best leader you can be, you must recognize how vital it is to create and maintain an environment that aligns with your personal and business goals.

Empowered by Epigenetics – Designing a Resilient Life

There is a powerful truth that every founder, leader, and visionary needs to understand on their path to sustainable success: the prescription for healing, growth, and high performance already exists within you. As much as the world tries to sell external solutions, lasting transformation happens from the inside out.

Enter epigenetics—the bridge between your biology and your behavior. This isn't just science; it's strategy. Epigenetics is the study of how our genes respond to environmental inputs by altering their expression. Think of your DNA as hardware and your daily habits as the software that tells it what to do. Just because you inherited a certain blueprint doesn't mean you're stuck with it. Through the lens of epigenetics, we now know that your environment, mindset, nutrition, and even your thoughts can switch genes on or off. That means you have the ability to influence your health, vitality, and even your emotional patterns through intentional choices.

This rewrites the old nature vs. nurture debate. It's not either/or—it's both. You may be born with a predisposition, but it's your lifestyle that determines whether those genes are expressed. Founders, who often live under immense stress, inconsistent routines, and poor sleep, are unknowingly creating an internal environment that either supports or sabotages their longevity. The good news? With knowledge comes agency. And that agency becomes power when put into practice.

Your Biology Listens to Your Lifestyle

Start with your environment. What you put on your skin, what you breathe, and what you eat is either triggering healing or harm. From glyphosate-laden produce to synthetic cleaning products, we are surrounded by invisible stressors. These environmental toxins are not neutral. They disrupt hormone function, impair cognitive clarity, and drive inflammation—all of which influence gene expression.

But just as toxins can hijack our health, small shifts can reverse the trend. Drinking filtered water. Swapping toxic cleaners for vinegar and essential oils. Choosing castile soap over commercial body wash. Saying no to plastic food containers and yes to glass. These aren't superficial lifestyle hacks—they are epigenetic interventions.

You Are Not Your Diagnosis

Understanding epigenetics gives you the freedom to detach from the narrative of genetic determinism. Whether it's a family history of heart disease or depression, you are not doomed. In fact, embracing practices like intermittent fasting, breathwork, or nutrient-dense eating can change how your body expresses its genes.

This is the invitation: take radical responsibility for your biology. Start seeing every choice as a signal to your body—a vote for who you want to become. Clean food, sunlight, community, rest, purpose, cold exposure, high-intensity training, and meditation all act like keys turning the dials of your genetic code in your favor.

In the rest of this chapter, we'll dive deeper into:

- How to detox your home and workspace
- Why your skincare routine matters as much as your workout
- What the science of hormesis reveals about "good stress"
- How trauma and thoughts influence your physiology
- A practical plan for upgrading your internal environment

The bottom line? You are more powerful than you think. Resilience isn't just a mindset—it's embedded in your biology. But only if you choose it.

How to Detox Your Home and Workspace

Your home and workspace are either supporting your vitality or silently eroding it. Detoxing these spaces doesn't require perfection—just intentionality. Start by swapping out the obvious culprits: toxic cleaning products, air fresheners, and plastic containers. Replace them with vinegar-based cleaners, essential oil diffusers, and glass storage.

Invest in an air purifier, especially if you live in a city or work in a sealed office. Open windows whenever possible. Use a water filter to remove chlorine, heavy metals, and pharmaceuticals from your tap. Upgrade your cookware to cast iron or stainless steel and ditch the non-stick pans, which release endocrine-disrupting chemicals into your food.

Your workspace matters, too. Clear clutter, add a few plants, and reduce EMF exposure by turning off Wi-Fi when not needed. Small daily exposures create cumulative biological stress—detoxing your environment is like exhaling the overwhelm so you can lead with clarity.

Why Your Skincare Routine Matters as Much as Your Workout

Your skin is your body's largest organ and a direct communication channel with your endocrine system. What you put on it matters. Most commercial skincare products contain endocrine disruptors like parabens, phthalates, and synthetic fragrances. These chemicals mimic hormones, confuse your body's signaling, and influence gene expression.

Swap conventional deodorants for aluminum-free versions. Choose mineral sunscreens over chemical-based ones. Use oils like jojoba, coconut, or shea butter instead of commercial lotions. Your skincare should be so clean you could eat it—because, in a way, your body does.

This isn't vanity—it's biochemistry. You can work out six days a week and still sabotage your health through daily chemical exposure. A founder's glow starts with clean inputs.

What the Science of Hormesis Reveals About "Good Stress"

Hormesis is the principle that small doses of stress can make you stronger. It's why lifting weights builds muscle and why intermittent fasting improves metabolic flexibility. The right kinds of stress—at the right dose—create adaptive responses that enhance resilience.

Cold showers or ice baths trigger mitochondrial biogenesis. Heat exposure through saunas boosts detoxification and brain-derived neurotrophic factor (BDNF). Fasting stimulates autophagy, clearing cellular waste. High-intensity training improves cardiovascular health and cognitive function.

The takeaway? Don't avoid all stress—learn to dose it wisely. Strategic discomfort is a growth tool when applied consciously. Hormetic stress builds the grit required for entrepreneurial endurance.

How Trauma and Thoughts Influence Your Physiology

Your body doesn't know the difference between a real threat and a perceived one. Chronic stress, negative thoughts, and unresolved trauma activate the same fight-or-flight responses as physical danger. Over time, this dysregulates cortisol, suppresses immune function, and alters gene expression.

Mindfulness, breathwork, journaling, and somatic therapy are not luxuries—they're necessities. Founders often override their own signals until the body forces a reset. Instead, choose proactive nervous system regulation. Rewire your brain's threat response with consistent mental hygiene, just like you would train your body.

Healing isn't just emotional—it's biological. Your genes listen to your beliefs.

A Practical Plan for Upgrading Your Internal Environment

1. **Audit your surroundings** – Use the Quick Guide to Detoxing Your Home to assess cleaning products, cookware, air and water quality, and personal care items.
2. **Upgrade your habits** – Add one hormetic practice to your routine: a daily walk in the cold, 12-hour fasts, or three sauna sessions a week.
3. **Regulate your stress** – Start with 5 minutes of breathwork daily. Write down three positive thoughts to replace the most common negative one.
4. **Track your inputs** – Keep a one-week log of what you put on your body and what goes in it. Awareness leads to agency.

5. **Create a founder-friendly environment** — Keep your workspace clean, well-lit, tech-balanced, and emotionally safe. Your nervous system thrives on order and simplicity.

The future of performance is personalized. And the path to resilience isn't just paved with ambition—it's grounded in biology. You get to shape your destiny, one cell at a time.

Building a Supportive Network

In addition to the physical environment, the social environment you create for yourself plays a significant role in your success. As a founder, your network is more than just a group of contacts; it is a support system that can offer guidance, collaboration, and encouragement through the inevitable ups and downs of entrepreneurship.

Your network influences your decisions, provides new perspectives, and helps you stay grounded during challenging times. Whether it's mentors, peers, or a dedicated team, your relationships are the backbone of your resilience.

The Importance of a Strong Support System

- Mentorship: Surrounding yourself with experienced mentors provides wisdom that can accelerate your growth. Their advice can help you avoid common pitfalls, guide you in difficult decision-making, and offer invaluable insights into leadership.
- Peers and Advisors: Connecting with other founders or business leaders who share similar experiences allows you to exchange ideas, problem-solve, and remain motivated. Having an advisory group made up of trusted

individuals can help provide diverse viewpoints and a sounding board for tough choices.

- Your Team: The success of your business is inextricably linked to the success of your team. A strong, aligned team that shares your values and vision will be essential in achieving long-term business success. Investing time in building relationships with your team members and fostering a collaborative culture will ensure you have the support you need to scale your business.

How to Cultivate a Supportive Network

- Seek Out Mentors: Whether formal or informal, finding a mentor who aligns with your values and has experience in the areas you seek guidance in can be a game-changer. Regular conversations with a mentor can offer perspectives you might not have considered.
- Join Founders Groups or Communities: Surround yourself with like-minded entrepreneurs through networking groups, masterminds, or online communities. These spaces allow you to share experiences, ask for help, and celebrate wins together.
- Foster Open Communication: Ensure that your team and network members feel comfortable sharing their ideas and concerns with you. Encouraging open, transparent communication will strengthen your relationships and foster a culture of collaboration and trust.

A strong support network can provide the emotional and professional resources you need to navigate the ups and downs of being a founder. The connections you nurture today will pay dividends in the future.

Setting Boundaries and Managing Relationships

One of the most challenging aspects of being a founder is balancing your personal life with the demands of your business. As an entrepreneur, you may often feel the pressure to be "always on," answering emails at odd hours or taking on too many responsibilities in an attempt to control everything. However, this approach can lead to burnout and negatively impact your relationships.

The ability to set clear boundaries is crucial for maintaining both your personal well-being and your business health. Boundaries help you prioritize your time, manage energy, and protect your mental and emotional health.

Why Boundaries Matter

- Protecting Your Time and Energy: Without boundaries, you risk over-committing to people or tasks that drain your resources. Setting clear limits ensures that you dedicate time to the things that matter most — your health, your family, and your business priorities.
- Preventing Burnout: Constantly working without respite leads to mental and physical exhaustion. Establishing boundaries around your work schedule, personal time, and relationships allows you to recharge and come back to your business with renewed energy and focus.
- Preserving Relationships: Without boundaries, you may find yourself neglecting important personal relationships in favor of business demands. By setting clear lines between work and personal life, you maintain the relationships that are key to your support system.

How to Set Healthy Boundaries

- Define Work and Personal Time: Decide when your workday starts and ends. Be disciplined about taking breaks and stepping away from work at the end of the day to recharge. Respect your own time, and others will follow suit.
- Learn to Say No: As a founder, you will receive numerous opportunities, requests, and demands on your time. Practice saying no to things that don't align with your core priorities or that would stretch you too thin. Saying no is a vital skill that ensures your energy goes toward your most important work.
- Communicate Clearly: Set expectations with your team, partners, and family members regarding your availability and time. Open communication about your boundaries ensures that everyone respects your needs.

By setting healthy boundaries, you create space for your personal life, protect your energy, and increase your ability to focus on your business goals with clarity and effectiveness.

Designing a Workspace That Inspires Creativity and Focus

Your physical workspace is one of the most influential aspects of your environment. It's where you spend the majority of your time thinking, creating, and making decisions. The design and organization of your workspace can impact your productivity, mood, and mental clarity.

A well-curated workspace supports your goals by providing a calm, efficient, and inspiring environment for you and your team. It fosters creativity, reduces distractions, and promotes a sense of well-being.

Key Elements of a Productive Workspace

- Natural Light: Exposure to natural light has been shown to increase energy levels, improve mood, and enhance focus. If possible, position your desk near a window or invest in good quality lighting to simulate daylight.
- Minimalism: A cluttered workspace can lead to mental clutter, making it harder to focus and stay productive. Adopt a minimalist approach, keeping only what you need on your desk. Use organizational tools like filing systems and storage boxes to keep things tidy.
- Inspiring Decor: Personalize your workspace with items that inspire and motivate you, whether that's artwork, meaningful objects, or plants. A space that reflects your personality and values can foster a sense of ownership and creativity.

Designing Your Perfect Workspace

- Ergonomics Matter: Invest in comfortable, ergonomic furniture that supports your posture and health. A well-designed chair, adjustable desk, and a proper keyboard setup can make a world of difference in your comfort and productivity.
- Create a "Focus Zone": Designate specific areas for specific activities. For example, have a space for deep work, one for brainstorming or creative activities, and another for collaborative meetings. When your workspace is organized for different tasks, your mind can shift more easily into the right mode.
- Control Noise: Noise can be a major distraction, so ensure your workspace allows for focus. This might mean investing in noise-canceling headphones or finding a quiet, private area to work.
- Turning notifications off on your phone is huge!

By designing a workspace that supports your needs and encourages focus, you create an environment where you can thrive and bring your best ideas to life.

Curating your environment for success is one of the most important steps you can take as a founder. Whether it's organizing your physical workspace, building a supportive network, setting boundaries, or understanding the impact of environmental factors on your well-being, your surroundings play a pivotal role in your performance and resilience.

CHAPTER 8
INTRODUCTION TO THE FOUR PILLARS

Overview of Mental, Physical, Spiritual, and Environmental Resilience

As a founder, navigating the complexities of running a business requires more than just business acumen and strategic planning. It demands a resilient approach—one that enables you to overcome challenges, stay focused under pressure, and maintain your drive even during tough times. Resilience isn't just about bouncing back from adversity; it's about thriving and growing stronger through the process.

The foundation of this resilience lies in Four Pillars that will guide you not only in building a successful business but also in leading a balanced and fulfilled life. These Four Pillars—Mental, Physical, Spiritual, and Environmental Resilience—work together, reinforcing one another, to ensure you are operating at your peak performance.

Each pillar provides a unique support system that, when strengthened, makes you more adaptable, focused, and effective in both personal and professional realms. By understanding and applying the principles of these Four Pillars, you can develop the holistic strength needed to succeed as a founder.

The Four Pillars of Founder Resilience

1. **Mental Resilience: Developing cognitive strength and the ability to focus, solve problems, and maintain clarity during challenging times.**
2. **Physical Resilience: Maintaining the energy, stamina, and health to keep up with the demands of entrepreneurship.**
3. **Spiritual Resilience: Connecting with your deeper sense of purpose and values, enabling you to lead with meaning and vision.**
4. **Environmental Resilience: Curating your surroundings—both physical and social—to optimize focus, productivity, and emotional well-being.**

Together, these pillars create a solid framework that nurtures your well-being and supports the growth of your business. By strengthening each pillar, you enhance your overall capacity to handle stress, make clear decisions, and stay aligned with your core mission.

How the Four Pillars Support Both Personal and Business Success

While these Four Pillars are distinct, they are interconnected. Each one influences the others, creating a synergy that fuels both personal growth and business success. Let's briefly explore how each pillar supports your journey as a founder:

1. **Mental Resilience**

   - Business Impact: As a founder, your decision-making skills are constantly tested. You need to have mental clarity to make critical choices, solve problems quickly, and stay calm under pressure. Mental resilience allows you to stay focused on your vision and lead with confidence, even in times of uncertainty.
   - Personal Impact: Mental resilience enables you to bounce back from setbacks and failures, maintaining a positive attitude and a solution-oriented mindset. This ability to stay mentally strong also improves your overall well-being, helping you navigate the stresses that come with being a founder.

2. **Physical Resilience**

   - Business Impact: Physical health is the foundation of your energy and stamina. Running a business can be demanding, and it requires a high level of energy to maintain momentum. Physical resilience ensures you have the endurance to lead through long hours, travel, and high-stress situations.
   - Personal Impact: When your physical health is strong, you feel more confident and capable. A regular fitness routine, balanced nutrition, and sufficient sleep contribute to your overall well-being, allowing you to feel your best, both personally and professionally.

3. **Spiritual Resilience**

   - Business Impact: Your connection to your deeper sense of purpose and values acts as a compass when faced with tough decisions. Spiritual resilience helps you stay true to your vision and mission, ensuring that your business grows in alignment with what matters most to you.

It fuels your passion and keeps you motivated during difficult times.

- **Personal Impact:** Spiritual resilience provides inner peace and clarity. By grounding yourself in your values, you gain a deeper sense of fulfillment and meaning, not just in your work but in all areas of your life. It allows you to cultivate a life that is rich in purpose and aligned with your true self.

4. **Environmental Resilience**

- **Business Impact:** Creating a supportive, productive work environment is essential for fostering creativity, innovation, and collaboration. A healthy company culture, coupled with a physical workspace that promotes focus and creativity, directly impacts the success of your business.

- **Personal Impact:** The environment you surround yourself with plays a major role in your emotional health and well-being. Whether it's your home office, your social network, or the people you interact with daily, a positive environment can increase your productivity, reduce stress, and improve your overall happiness.

Each of these pillars contributes to your ability to lead with resilience, navigate challenges, and find long-term success. While they may seem separate at first glance, they are deeply interconnected—your mental clarity depends on your physical energy, your spiritual purpose informs your business vision, and your environment influences both your emotional state and work performance.

Resilience Deficiencies

Symptoms of Low Mental Resilience:

Mental resilience refers to one's ability to adapt and recover from adversity or significant sources of stress. Poor mental resilience can manifest differently across the various domains of life. Here are some potential symptoms as they relate to health, wealth, career/business, and relationships:

Health:

- Physical Symptoms: Frequent illnesses, headaches, fatigue, digestive problems, and sleep disturbances can be indicative of stress or poor coping mechanisms.
- Neglecting Self-care: Avoidance of regular check-ups, poor diet choices, lack of exercise, and ignoring medical advice.
- Substance Abuse: Over-reliance on alcohol, drugs, or medication as a coping mechanism.

Economics:

- Impulsive Spending: Using shopping as a coping mechanism or making financial decisions without adequate forethought.
- Avoiding Financial Responsibilities: Ignoring bills, evading conversations about money, or lacking the discipline to save.
- Risk Avoidance: Being overly fearful of making any investment or taking calculated financial risks.

Relationships:

- Procrastination: Regularly delaying tasks or decision-making, leading to inefficiencies.
- Lack of Motivation: Feeling disinterested or detached from work, even if it was previously enjoyable.
- Avoidance Behavior: Steering clear of challenging tasks or confrontations with colleagues.

- Increased Absenteeism: Taking more sick days or showing up late regularly.

Opportunities:

- Isolation: Avoiding social events, family gatherings, or spending time with friends.
- Heightened Sensitivity: Taking offense easily, being overly defensive, or misinterpreting neutral statements as negative.
- Communication Breakdown: Struggling to express feelings, keeping things bottled up, or avoiding conflict entirely.
- Dependency: Over-relying on a partner, friend, or family member for emotional support to an unhealthy extent.

It's essential to note that everyone can exhibit some of these symptoms from time to time, and it doesn't always indicate a lack of mental resilience. However, if these behaviors are persistent, it might suggest that one's ability to cope with stress or adversity is compromised. In such cases, it can be beneficial to seek guidance or counseling to develop coping strategies and build mental resilience.

Symptoms of Low Physical Resilience:

Physical resilience refers to the body's ability to adapt to challenges, recover from injuries or illnesses, and maintain optimum health over time. When physical resilience is compromised, it can manifest in various ways across the domains of life:

Health:

- Frequent Illnesses: Catching colds or infections more often than usual.

- Slow Recovery: Taking longer to heal from injuries or illnesses.
- Chronic Fatigue: Constantly feeling tired or lacking energy, even after ample rest.
- Reduced Physical Endurance: Running out of breath quickly or experiencing a rapid decline in stamina during physical activities.

Economic:

- Medical Expenses: Incurring frequent medical bills due to regular visits to healthcare providers.
- Insurance Premiums: Potential rise in health insurance premiums due to frequent claims or identified health risks.
- Reduced Earning Potential: Being unable to work as consistently or efficiently due to health issues.

Relationships:

- Increased Absenteeism: Missing work frequently due to health-related issues.
- Reduced Productivity: Not being able to perform at the expected level, possibly leading to missed promotions or job opportunities.
- Lack of Adaptability: Struggling with tasks that demand physical exertion or dexterity.

Opportunities:

- Avoidance of Social Activities: Missing out on social events or gatherings due to physical discomfort or limitations.
- Dependency: Relying excessively on loved ones for daily tasks or activities.

- Strained Relationships: Loved ones might feel the burden or stress of the individual's recurrent health issues, leading to potential relationship strains.

Recognizing these signs early and seeking intervention—whether it's through physical therapy, lifestyle modifications, or medical guidance—can help in building and restoring physical resilience. As with mental resilience, everyone has moments of physical vulnerability, but persistent symptoms might indicate a deeper issue.

Symptoms of Low Spiritual Resilience:

Spiritual resilience refers to the ability to maintain or regain a sense of inner peace, purpose, and connection, especially in the face of challenges or crises. It encompasses beliefs, values, and a deeper understanding of one's place in the world, whether these come from religious beliefs, personal values, or a broader sense of the universe. When spiritual resilience is compromised, it can manifest in various ways across different domains of life:

Health:

- Psychosomatic Symptoms: Experiencing physical symptoms that might be rooted in spiritual or emotional distress, like unexplained aches or fatigue.
- Emotional Disturbances: Feelings of persistent sadness, anxiety, or emptiness without a clear external cause.
- Loss of Routine: Neglecting practices that previously supported well-being, like meditation, prayer, or other rituals.

Economics:

- Misalignment with Values: Making financial decisions that conflict with personal or spiritual beliefs, leading to regret or guilt.

- Overemphasis on Materialism: Relying excessively on material possessions for happiness, potentially leading to overspending or financial strain.
- Generosity Burnout: Giving beyond one's means due to a sense of spiritual or moral obligation, leading to financial strain.

Relationships:

- Lack of Fulfillment: Feeling a sense of emptiness or meaninglessness in one's work, even if it's successful on paper.
- Moral Conflicts: Experiencing distress when work demands conflict with personal or spiritual values.
- Isolation: Feeling disconnected or isolated from colleagues, especially if they don't share or understand one's spiritual beliefs or values.

Opportunities:

- Spiritual Isolation: Feeling misunderstood or alone in one's spiritual journey, leading to potential isolation from friends or family.
- Value Conflicts: Experiencing tensions in relationships due to differing spiritual beliefs or moral values.
- Over-dependency: Relying too heavily on spiritual or religious leaders, groups, or partners for validation or direction, stifling personal growth.

Building and maintaining spiritual resilience often involves regular reflection, engaging in spiritual practices, seeking community or guidance, and ensuring alignment between one's actions and beliefs. It's also about recognizing and respecting that spiritual journeys are deeply personal and can vary greatly among individuals. If someone feels a loss of spiritual resilience, seeking guidance from spiritual mentors, counselors, or communities can be beneficial.

Symptoms of Low Environmental Resilience:

While environmental resilience often involves broader systems and ecosystems, there are behaviors and choices at the individual and community level that can either support or degrade this resilience. When our behaviors are not conducive to fostering environmental resilience, the negative repercussions can manifest in various domains of life. Here are some symptoms or consequences of poor environmental resilience traits we might exhibit:

Health:

- Nutritional Deficiencies: Without access to healthy food, individuals might face health issues related to malnutrition, such as weakened immune systems, fatigue, and increased susceptibility to diseases.
- Mental Health Strains: Limited access to nature and constantly being in toxin-laden environments can increase stress, anxiety, and feelings of confinement or claustrophobia.
- Physical Health Issues: Living in areas with a high environmental toxin load can lead to respiratory problems, allergies, and other health complications.

Economics:

- Restricted Economic Growth: A lack of socioeconomic mobility means individuals can't move up the economic ladder, leading to generational poverty.
- Healthcare Costs: Increased health issues due to a poor environment mean higher medical bills, straining individual and community finances.

- Dependency: Without resources and opportunities, there's a greater dependency on welfare systems or aid, leading to a cycle of financial stagnation.

Relationships:

- Stifled Opportunities: Individuals might have fewer job opportunities or avenues for business growth due to a lack of resources, connections, or opportunities in their immediate environment.
- Decreased Productivity: Poor health, stemming from environmental factors, can lead to increased absenteeism or reduced efficiency at work.
- Lack of Innovation: A static environment with limited socioeconomic movement can dampen creativity and entrepreneurial spirit.

Opportunities:

- Social Isolation: Without a strong social network or sense of tribal connection, individuals might feel alone, unsupported, or misunderstood.
- Interpersonal Conflicts: Differences in values, goals, or the perception of communal resources can lead to conflicts within the community.
- Lack of Collective Identity: Without pride in a shared heritage or common ground, community bonds can weaken, leading to fragmentation and individual isolation.

Our connection to each other is something that unites us all, serving as the foundation on which to build resilient individuals and communities.

Building Resilience: The Holistic Approach

The concept of resilience goes beyond simply "bouncing back" from hardship; it's about proactively building strength in all areas of your life. By adopting a holistic approach to resilience, you can ensure that you are operating at your fullest potential, ready to handle any challenge that comes your way.

It's important to remember that resilience is not a fixed trait; it is a skill that can be developed over time. Like a muscle, it requires consistent effort and attention. In the chapters that follow, we will explore how to build mental, physical, spiritual, and environmental resilience in practical ways. Each section will offer actionable strategies, tools, and insights to help you strengthen the specific areas that will have the greatest impact on your success.

The key is to focus on continuous improvement. Building resilience is an ongoing process. It requires a willingness to learn, adapt, and make small changes that compound over time. As you strengthen each of these pillars, you'll see exponential growth not just in your business, but also in your personal life.

MBSE Resilience Clarity Worksheet

In order to develop a sense of clarity around your own levels of mental, physical, spiritual and environmental assets of resilience, using a scale from 1-5 where 1 is the least you identify with a characteristic and 5 being one you believe you have mastered, number each of the characteristics in each of these sections. Once you are finished go ahead and add your totals for each section.

Introduction to the four pillars

Mental Resilience Characteristics

A resilient mindset is one that is capable of maintaining both cognitive and executive function, regardless of external stress factors. Further, it is the ability to adapt to any challenging environment (whether this be internal or external), while still maintaining optimal function and focus on a set of objective(s). This adaptability is comprised of the following elements:

Characteristics of a Resilient Mind

Overcoming Fear

- Comfortable with new or "stretching" situations
- Welcomes change
- Not being afraid of failure
- Growth Mindset
- Grit

Self Confidence

- Self-esteem
- Assertiveness
- Patience

Self Efficacy

- Reliable
- Self Reliance
- Goal Oriented
- Work ethic

Self Determination

- Self-Worth

- Emotional control
- Self Control
- **Total/75**
    - **0-25** Needs significant improvement
    - **26-50** Off to a good start, just needs a little support
    - **51-75** Crushing it, has most of the assets needed for greatness

Welcome to the journey of developing your mental resilience! This worksheet will help you explore the core aspects of mental resilience and provide insights into your personal strengths and areas for growth. As you go through each section, reflect on your responses and consider how you can enhance your mental resilience over time.

Overcoming Fear – Embracing Growth

In order to overcome fear we must challenge ourselves to expose ourselves to those activities or situations that stretch us beyond our comfort zones. It can be seen as either a threat or an opportunity for growth. Think about instances where you faced challenges recently:

1. Have you ever viewed a challenge as an opportunity for learning and personal development?
2. Have you ever avoided a challenge due to discomfort or fear of the unknown?

Mentally tough individuals embrace challenges, regardless of the outcome, as opportunities for valuable learning experiences. On the other hand, those who are mentally sensitive tend to avoid challenges due to negative experiences associated with them.

Self Discipline – Building Inner Strength

Self Determination gives us the confidence to believe in your abilities and your ability to stand strong in the face of setbacks. Reflect on situations where your self determination played a role:

1. Have you faced setbacks with determination, seeing them as part of life's journey?
2. Do you find it challenging to maintain your confidence when faced with criticism or opposition?

Mentally tough individuals accept setbacks as part of life and maintain their confidence even in challenging circumstances. Mentally sensitive individuals may feel defeated by setbacks and struggle to maintain their confidence.

Self Determination – Pursuing Goals

Commitment involves making and keeping promises, both to yourself and others. Think about your approach to commitments:

1. Do you break down goals into manageable steps and celebrate your commitment's success?
2. Do you find yourself avoiding commitments due to fear of failure or intimidation?

Mentally tough individuals break down goals, maintain focus, and celebrate successes. Mentally sensitive individuals might avoid commitments due to fear of failure or intimidation.

The Fourth C of Mental Toughness: Control – Shaping Your Life

Control refers to how much you feel in control of your life and emotions. Reflect on your feelings of control:

1. Do you manage your emotions well, especially during stressful situations?
2. Do you tend to express your emotions openly or internalize them?

Mentally tough individuals are skilled at managing emotions, maintaining calm in crisis, and revealing emotions selectively. Mentally sensitive individuals may struggle to control their emotions and feel overwhelmed in stressful situations.

As you delve into the components of mental resilience, remember that growth is a gradual process. Recognize your strengths and areas for improvement, and know that building mental resilience is about developing skills that will serve you well throughout your life. Use this self-assessment as a starting point for your journey towards greater mental toughness and resilience.

Physical Resilience Characteristics

A resilient body is one that is robustly immune to disease, infection, and mental dysfunction despite exposure to various stressors.

Characteristics of a Resilient Body

- High functioning healthy immune system
- Good cardiovascular health
- Resilience to physical discomfort or injury (physical)

- Healthy relationship with food
- High HRV values
- **Total/25**

    - **0-9** Needs significant improvement
    - **10-17** Off to a good start, just needs a little support
    - **18-25** Crushing it, has most of the assets needed for greatness

The two biggest levers that we can pull to improve our physical resilience is how we move our bodies and what we put in it, namely; exercise and nutrition.

Spiritual Resilience Characteristics

Spiritual resilience is the ability to sustain one's sense of self and purpose through a set of beliefs, principles or values while encountering adversity, stress, and trauma by using internal and external spiritual resources.

Characteristics of a Resilient Spirit

- Understanding the Ego
- Emotional regulation
- Courage
- Vulnerability
- Strong sense of self worth
- Belief in one's self.
- Believing in something greater than themselves
- Gratitude
- Happiness
- **Total/45**

- **0-15** Needs significant improvement
- **16-30** Off to a good start, just needs a little support
- **31-45** Crushing it, has most of the assets needed for greatness

External Forces of Resilience

Environment: An environment that fosters resilience is one with access to nature, low toxin load, and individuals that have your best interests in mind.

Characteristics of a Resilience promoting environment

- Access to healthy food
- Access to Nature
- Strong social network
- Low environmental toxin
- Socioeconomic motility
- Identifying with and Participation in ones tribe
- **Total/30**

  - **0-10** Needs significant improvement
  - **11-20** Off to a good start, just needs a little support
  - **21-30** Crushing it, has most of the assets needed for greatness

Community: a resilient community is one with shared cultural beliefs, a historical common ground, where rituals, and valued resources are willingly shared amongst the group, empowering individuals to face more than what they could on their own.

Tribal Resiliency comes from:

- Positive support system
- People that are pursuing similar goals
- Vulnerability
- Pride in heritage or shared common ground/struggles

Origin of The Four Domains of Resiliency

Resiliency is one of the most critical skills for anyone aiming to thrive in demanding environments, and for founders, it is nothing short of essential. It refers to the ability to recover from challenges, adapt to change, and continue moving forward despite setbacks. For founders, who operate in the volatile and high-pressure world of entrepreneurship, resiliency can mean the difference between success and failure. To grasp its importance fully, we must delve into the origins of the four domains of resiliency—health, economics, relationships, and opportunities—and uncover how they underpin what is often referred to as "founder mode." This unique mindset encapsulates the relentless drive, creativity, and adaptability required to launch and lead a business.

Origins of the Four Domains of Resilience

1. **Health Resilience** Imagine trying to run a business while constantly exhausted or battling stress. Health resiliency, rooted in health sciences and physiology, emphasizes the importance of maintaining physical and mental well-being. Hans Selye's research on stress, particularly his general adaptation syndrome (GAS), laid the groundwork for understanding how the body responds to and recovers from stress.

For founders, sustaining health resiliency means committing to practices like regular exercise, adequate sleep, and balanced nutrition—habits that recharge the body and sharpen the mind. Mental health, too, plays a pivotal role. Mindfulness, meditation, and stress management techniques empower individuals to manage the inevitable pressures of entrepreneurship, enabling them to remain calm, focused, and productive.

2. **Economic Resilience** Wealth resiliency isn't just about accumulating money; it's about mastering the art of financial adaptability. Entrepreneurs often face fluctuating incomes, unpredictable markets, and tight budgets. This domain, grounded in financial planning and behavioral finance, highlights the importance of making strategic financial decisions to weather economic storms.

   Founders who build wealth resiliency develop robust financial plans, establish emergency funds, and master budgeting and risk management. By embracing a proactive approach to financial health, they can ensure their ventures remain viable, even in times of uncertainty. This domain isn't just a safety net—it's a launching pad for sustainable growth and opportunity.

3. **Relationship Resiliency** Founders may shoulder many responsibilities, but success is rarely achieved alone. Relationship resiliency—the ability to build and sustain meaningful connections—is a critical asset. Rooted in sociology and social psychology, this domain highlights the role of social bonds in fostering emotional and practical support.

   Whether it's leaning on mentors, collaborating with peers, or fostering a strong organizational culture, relationship resiliency empowers founders to navigate challenges with confidence and clarity. By nurturing trust, practicing effective communication, and valuing diverse perspectives, they create networks that uplift and strengthen their ventures. Strong relationships are not just a resource—they're a foundation for innovation and resilience.

4. **Opportunity Resilience** No founder's journey is without its share of setbacks. Whether facing a shifting market, unexpected competition, or internal challenges, career and business resiliency enables founders to adapt, innovate, and lead effectively. This domain draws from organizational behavior and entrepreneurship research, emphasizing strategic thinking and persistence.

Founders who cultivate business resiliency are willing to pivot when necessary, embrace continuous learning, and build strong professional networks. Innovation and flexibility are their cornerstones, allowing them to turn obstacles into opportunities and keep their ventures on course. By staying adaptable and future-focused, they transform challenges into stepping stones for success.

Relating the Four Domains of Resilience to Founder Mode

To truly appreciate the power of these domains, consider their application to founder mode—the mindset of navigating entrepreneurship's relentless demands.

1. **Health Resilience in Founder Mode** Founders often work long hours and face immense stress, making health resiliency a priority. By taking care of their physical and mental well-being, they can sustain the energy and focus needed to lead effectively. Incorporating wellness practices isn't a luxury; it's a necessity for long-term success.
2. **Wealth Resilience in Founder Mode** Financial uncertainty is an inevitable part of entrepreneurship. Found-

ers with strong wealth resiliency have the tools to manage cash flow, adapt to market changes, and invest wisely. They recognize that financial health is as much about preparation as it is about opportunity.

3. **Career/Business Resilience in Founder Mode** The entrepreneurial landscape is constantly shifting, and adaptability is key. Founders who embrace career resiliency are not afraid to take risks, pivot strategies, or seek new knowledge. This flexibility keeps them ahead of the curve and positions them for sustained growth.

4. **Relationship Resilience in Founder Mode** Building a business is as much about people as it is about ideas. Founders with strong relationship resiliency create environments of trust, collaboration, and mutual respect. They know that a supportive network can provide fresh perspectives, emotional backing, and practical solutions when challenges arise.

Resiliency is not a static trait but a dynamic framework that encompasses health, economic factors, relationships, and business opportunities. By understanding the origins of these domains and their critical role in founder mode, entrepreneurs can unlock the tools to thrive in even the most challenging circumstances. Resilience isn't just about surviving—it's about flourishing, leading with purpose, and creating lasting impact. Whether you're a seasoned founder or just beginning your entrepreneurial journey, mastering these domains will equip you to face adversity head-on and emerge stronger every time.

The HERO Framework for Resilience: Redefining Strength Across Life's Four Core Domains

Resilience is not a single trait—it's a system. A web of interdependent strengths that, when nurtured, support us in navigating adversity, adapting to change, and thriving in our pursuit of purpose. In this program, we use the HERO framework—Health, Economics, Relationships, and Opportunities—to help founders assess and build resilience in the areas that matter most.

Each domain impacts the others. When your health improves, your performance at work follows. When your finances are stable, your relationships have room to deepen. When your relationships are strong, you're more likely to spot and seize new opportunities. True resilience is built when all four HERO domains are addressed holistically.

To get clear on where you are today, take time to assess yourself in each HERO domain using the MBSE lens (Mental, Physical, Spiritual, and Environmental). For each trait listed under the domain categories below, rate yourself from 1 to 5—1 being "this needs attention" and 5 being "I've mastered this."

Health

MBSE Score: _____ **(combine totals)**

- **Resilient Mind**
    - **Comfortable with stretching situations**
    - **Welcomes change**
    - **Grit and growth mindset**
    - **Confidence and assertiveness**

- Self-worth and emotional control
- Patience, reliability, and self-reliance
- Commitment and goal orientation

- **Resilient Body**
  - Strong immune function
  - Cardiovascular health
  - Resilience to discomfort or injury
  - High HRV (Heart Rate Variability)
  - Healthy relationship with food

- **Resilient Spirit**
  - Emotional regulation and self-belief
  - Courage and vulnerability
  - Understanding the ego
  - Belief in something greater
  - Gratitude and happiness

- **Resilient Environment**
  - Access to nature and healthy food
  - Low exposure to toxins
  - Strong social networks and community

Economics (Wealth)

MBSE Score: _____ (combine totals)

- **Resilient Mind**
  - Self-discipline in money management
  - Confidence in financial decision-making

- Willingness to take calculated risks
- Clarity around short- and long-term goals
- Resilience through setbacks

- **Resilient Body**
  - Energy and stamina for productivity
  - Health behaviors that reduce medical expenses
  - Awareness of physical signs of financial stress

- **Resilient Spirit**
  - Belief in one's ability to generate and manage wealth
  - Sense of purpose tied to financial decisions
  - Gratitude for what one has

- **Resilient Environment**
  - Socioeconomic mobility
  - Access to mentors or financial literacy resources
  - Connection to community financial resources

Relationships

MBSE Score: _____ (combine totals)

- **Resilient Mind**
  - Emotional intelligence
  - Boundaries and communication skills
  - Self-awareness in conflict

- Clarity around personal values and expectations
- **Resilient Body**
  - Physical energy to invest in others
  - Regulation of stress and hormones affecting mood
- **Resilient Spirit**
  - Vulnerability and empathy
  - Ability to receive love and support
  - Emotional reciprocity
- **Resilient Environment**
  - Supportive inner circle
  - Exposure to people who challenge and elevate you
  - Safe environments for growth and openness

Opportunities (Career/Business/Calling)

MBSE Score: _____ (combine totals)

- **Resilient Mind**
  - Clarity in vision and strategic thinking
  - Ability to take action in uncertainty
  - Adaptability to industry changes
  - Learning mindset and resourcefulness
- **Resilient Body**

- Energy and presence in high-stakes environments
- Physical health supporting productivity and leadership

- **Resilient Spirit**
  - Deep alignment with your mission
  - Courage to pursue what matters
  - Optimism about your path forward

- **Resilient Environment**
  - Access to mentors, peers, and collaborators
  - Clean, focused workspace
  - Opportunities for continued learning

Step 1: Define Your Top 5 Priorities in Each H.E.R.O. Domain

Take a moment to reflect on your current strengths, weaknesses, and areas for growth. Below, list your top five priorities for each domain, focusing on what will most significantly impact your personal and business success.

Health (Physical & Mental Well-being)

1. _____
2. _____
3. _____
4. _____
5. _____

Example: Prioritizing sleep, daily exercise, stress management, balanced nutrition, and mental clarity through meditation.

Economics (Wealth Resilience & Financial Stability)

1. _____
2. _____
3. _____
4. _____
5. _____

Example: Increasing cash flow, reducing debt, diversifying investments, improving financial literacy, and leveraging Bitcoin for long-term financial security.

Relationships (Personal & Professional Network)

1. _____
2. _____
3. _____
4. _____
5. _____

Example: Strengthening family bonds, networking with mentors, improving communication skills, deepening business partnerships, and engaging in community support.

Opportunities (Business & Career Growth)

1. _____
2. _____
3. _____

4. _____
5. _____

Example: Expanding market reach, developing new products, improving leadership skills, leveraging emerging technologies, and mastering digital marketing strategies.

Step 2: Select Your #1 Priority in Each Domain

From your top five, select the **single most important focus area** in each category that will drive the greatest long-term impact.

- **Health Priority:** _____
- **Economics Priority:** _____
- **Relationships Priority:** _____
- **Opportunities Priority:** _____

Before moving on to the next chapter, take a moment to review the results from your H.E.R.O Plan in Chapter 1.

CHAPTER 9
MENTAL RESILIENCE — FOUNDATIONAL THINKING FOR PURPOSE-DRIVEN SUCCESS

As a founder, your ability to make decisions under pressure, adapt to uncertainty, and lead with clarity is one of your greatest assets. Mental resilience isn't just about grit—it's about building a thinking toolkit that allows you to solve problems, anticipate obstacles, and pivot with purpose. That toolkit begins with mental models.

Mental models are cognitive frameworks—ways of understanding the world and making sense of complex situations. As James Clear, author of **Atomic Habits**, puts it: "A mental model is an explanation of how something works... any sort of concept, framework, or worldview that you carry around in your mind." For purpose-driven founders, mental models are the scaffolding for sound strategy, emotional regulation, and breakthrough innovation.

Inversion: Thinking Backwards to Move Forward

Inversion flips traditional problem-solving on its head. Instead of asking, "How can I succeed?" inversion prompts you to ask, "What would guarantee my failure?" By identifying the biggest risks, you reveal what to avoid—and therefore what to focus on.

Founder Application: Want to increase customer retention by 50%? Ask: What would drive customers away?

- Poor support
- Ignored feedback
- Overpromising, underdelivering
- Low product quality

Now invert it:

- Provide stellar customer service
- Build feedback loops
- Set and meet realistic expectations
- Focus on quality and consistency

Founder Reflection: Choose a key metric or outcome you're working on. What would lead to failure? Invert those factors into a new action plan.

First Principles Thinking: Rebuild from the Ground Up

Popularized by Elon Musk, first principles thinking encourages breaking problems down to their most basic truths, then reasoning upward from there. This model is especially powerful for founders trying to innovate beyond the status quo.

Founder Application: Scaling your business? Instead of copying other startups, define what scaling means for *you*.

- What are the core components? (Capacity, efficiency, quality)
- Which assumptions can be challenged? (Do I really need more staff—or smarter automation?)

Founder Reflection: Take a current challenge in your business and break it down to its raw elements. What assumptions can you question? What creative solutions emerge?

Second-Order Thinking: Look Past the First Move

First-order thinking evaluates the immediate result of a decision. Second-order thinking examines the longer-term ripple effects.

Founder Application: Considering deep discounts to boost sales?

- First-order effect: More customers now.
- Second-order effects:
  - Loyal customers may feel cheated
  - New customers might only buy on discount
  - Your brand may be devalued

Second-order thinking keeps your business resilient by ensuring short-term gains don't become long-term setbacks.

Founder Reflection: Map out a major decision. What are the second- and third-order effects? Are they worth the initial benefit?

Occam's Razor: Simplicity Wins

Occam's Razor suggests that the simplest solution—when all things are equal—is often the best. Complexity is the enemy of execution.

Founder Application: When developing a new feature, ask:

- What's the minimum viable version that solves the problem?
- Are we adding complexity that confuses the user?

Founder Reflection: Review your core offering. What can be simplified without reducing value?

Hanlon's Razor: Don't Assume Malice

Hanlon's Razor reminds us: "Never attribute to malice what can be explained by incompetence or miscommunication." This mental model helps founders lead with empathy.

Founder Application: If a team member underperforms:

- Were expectations clear?
- Did they have what they needed?
- Is something happening in their personal life?

Founder Reflection: Think of a recent conflict. How can this model shift your perspective and improve how you handle similar situations in the future?

Cognitive Dissonance: Turn Discomfort into Change

When beliefs and behaviors clash, we experience dissonance. Rather than avoiding it, founders can harness it.

Founder Application: If your company values transparency but your team hesitates to speak openly, that tension reveals a gap worth addressing. Realigning action with values builds trust and long-term culture.

Founder Reflection: Where do your actions or your company's culture contradict your values? What needs to shift?

Trauma and Challenge: Using Pain as Fuel

Every founder faces adversity. But with the right mindset, trauma can become the catalyst for growth.

- Reframe failure: See it as necessary feedback.
- Build support systems: Lean on community, mentors, and coaching.
- Integrate adversity: Make meaning from setbacks. Turn your scar into your story.

Founder Reflection: What past hardship shaped your resilience? How can you use that experience as fuel for the next chapter?

The Power of Deliberate Decision-Making

Your decisions shape your destiny—and your company's future. With every choice, you either reinforce resilience or invite regression. The mental models in this chapter are not meant to be memorized, but practiced. Each one is a lens, helping you see more clearly and act more effectively.

The world doesn't need more reactive founders. It needs leaders who think deliberately, reflect deeply, and respond with courage. Start where you are. Choose one model and apply it to a challenge this week.

Your trajectory changes with how you think—and what you do next.

Your hero's journey begins with clarity of mind.

Make it count.

Unlocking Flow, Focus, and the Founder's Edge

Mental resilience isn't just about enduring hardship—it's about designing your mental operating system to support peak performance under pressure. One of the most powerful manifestations of this resilience is the ability to enter flow states: those moments of complete immersion where productivity, creativity, and purpose align.

For founders, flow is not a luxury—it's a necessity. In the chaos of building, scaling, and leading, your ability to block out noise and tap into deep, focused work determines how far and how fast you go. And yet, achieving flow requires more than willpower. It demands an intentional environment, a sharp mindset, and habits designed for clarity.

How to Enter a Flow State

1. **Clear Goals**

   A foggy brain can't focus. When your goals are specific and achievable, your mind is free to fully engage. Before you sit down to work, ask: What does success look like for this session?

2. **Challenge-Skill Balance**

   Flow lives at the edge of discomfort. If the task is too easy, you get bored. Too hard, and you get overwhelmed. Aim for a sweet spot where the challenge stretches your skills but remains within reach.

3. **Eliminate Distractions**

   Turn off notifications. Set boundaries. Use time blocks. Your phone, inbox, and Slack are flow killers—build barriers to guard your focus.

4. **Practice Presence**

   Mindfulness strengthens your attention muscle. Meditation, breathwork, or even mindful walking can train your brain to stay centered, which makes entering flow faster and more reliable.

Founder Flow in Action: Real-Life Examples

Alex Hormozi — Known for his deep work routines, Alex blocks time for high-leverage tasks, eliminates notifications, and works in distraction-free zones. His secret: ruthless simplicity and prioritization.

Elon Musk — Schedules his day in 5-minute blocks to maintain focus while switching between companies. He dedicates entire sessions to engineering and problem-solving with singular intent.

Tim Ferriss — Uses the 80/20 rule and task batching. His mornings start with meditation, journaling, and movement to prime the mind for deep work.

Marie Forleo — Creates theme-based days and starts each morning with creative output before distractions begin. She integrates movement and play to sustain mental energy.

Sara Blakely – Finds flow in solitude. Whether it's silent drives or journaling sessions, she makes space for uninterrupted thought and creative strategy.

Visualization: Training the Brain for Success

Flow isn't just something you fall into—it's something you can rehearse. Visualization is a powerful tool used by high performers across disciplines to prime the mind and enhance focus.

Why It Works

Visualization activates the same neural circuits as real experience. It reinforces belief, builds emotional resilience, and strengthens focus through mental rehearsal.

How to Practice

- **Quiet Space**: Eliminate external noise. Get still.
- **Visualize Success**: See yourself achieving your goal. Make it vivid.
- **Feel the Emotion**: Embody the pride, joy, and fulfillment.
- **Reinforce with Affirmations**: Speak your identity into existence.

   Example: Serena Williams visualizes her matches in vivid detail, including the emotions she'll feel when she wins. That mental repetition strengthens her confidence when pressure hits.

Build Flow Into Your Routine

The 5-Minute Focus Drill: Set a timer. Focus on one task. When your mind wanders, gently return. Build from 5 minutes to 20. It's a workout for your attention span.

The Daily Visualization Practice: Each morning, visualize your #1 goal. Picture success. Rehearse the win. Pair it with affirmations. Start your day already in flow.

Seneca and the Power of Purposeful Focus

Ancient wisdom meets modern resilience. Seneca wrote: *"It's not about how long you live; it's about how well you live."* In the founder world, this means your hours don't matter if they're wasted.

Don't just fill your day. Ask:

- Am I moving the needle?
- Is this task aligned with my greater purpose?
- What's the one thing I can do today that makes everything else easier or unnecessary?

Seneca's strategy is simple but profound: focus on what matters, let go of what doesn't. This is how founders build not just successful companies, but meaningful lives.

Mental Resilience = Leadership Clarity

At the heart of every founder's journey is the mind—the driver of decisions, the anchor in chaos, the architect of vision. By developing mental models, practicing deep focus, leveraging visualization, and designing for flow, you gain a secret edge:

Clarity. Confidence. Calm.

Mental resilience isn't just a skill—it's the operating system for the founder's life. Master it, and you don't just survive the entrepreneurial journey—you thrive with purpose.

Mental Simulation Exercise and Reflection

Box Breathing for Alpha Wave Relaxation

As a founder, the pressure to constantly innovate, manage, and perform can feel overwhelming. But what if you could reset your mind in just a few minutes, gain clarity, and sharpen your decision-making edge? Box breathing, or square breathing, is a proven technique to reduce stress and help your brain enter a calm yet focused state, often associated with alpha brain waves. Here's how you can use this simple yet transformative method to unlock your best self during high-pressure moments or when preparing for critical tasks.

Why Box Breathing Works for Founders

Founders often juggle a whirlwind of responsibilities. This mental load can trigger a fight-or-flight response, clouding judgment and sapping creativity. Box breathing counteracts this by regulating your nervous system, restoring balance, and priming your brain for peak performance.

When practiced regularly, this exercise helps you:

- Stay calm during high-stakes situations.
- Improve focus for strategic thinking.
- Transition from reactive to proactive decision-making.

Let's dive into the steps to master this powerful tool.

Step-by-Step Guide to Box Breathing

Step 1: Create Your Zone of Focus

- Sit or lie down in a comfortable position where you won't be interrupted.
- Close your eyes to block out distractions and imagine stepping into your "focus zone"—a mental space where you feel in control and capable.

Step 2: Align Your Posture

- Keep your back straight but relaxed.
- Let your shoulders drop, unclench your jaw, and rest your hands naturally. Picture tension leaving your body like a balloon slowly deflating.

Step 3: Inhale Deeply (Count to Four)

- Breathe in slowly through your nose for a count of four. Feel the air filling your lungs, expanding your chest and diaphragm.
- Visualize this breath as energy or light fueling your clarity and purpose.

Step 4: Hold the Breath (Count to Four)

- Hold your breath for four counts. Think of this pause as a moment to reset—like hitting the "save" button on your focus.

Step 5: Exhale Slowly (Count to Four)

- Gently exhale through your mouth for four counts. Imagine releasing stress, doubts, or mental clutter with each breath.

Step 6: Pause Again (Count to Four)

- Before your next breath, pause for four counts. Embrace the stillness and reflect on the calm you're cultivating.

Step 7: Repeat the Cycle

- Continue this breathing pattern for 4–5 minutes. If your mind starts to wander, gently guide it back to the rhythm of your breath.

Advanced Tips

Gradual Lengthening

- Once you've mastered the basic cycle, extend the count to six or eight for a deeper relaxation effect.

Visualization Techniques

- During each phase of the breath, picture scenarios that inspire confidence: nailing a pitch, leading your team with clarity, or celebrating a major milestone.

Anchor to Routine

- Practice box breathing during moments when stress tends to peak—before a presentation, after an intense meeting, or when brainstorming new ideas.

Reflection and Alpha State Awareness

- After completing a session, take a moment to reflect: How has your mindset shifted? Are your thoughts clearer? Do you feel more balanced?
- Recognize this calm-yet-alert mental state as your alpha brain wave mode—the sweet spot for problem-solving and innovation.

Challenge:

Try box breathing twice daily for a week. Journal your experience, noting any changes in your energy, focus, or ability to handle challenges. How does this simple habit reshape your approach to founder life?

Box breathing isn't just a relaxation technique; it's a strategic tool for founders looking to operate at their best. By mastering your breath, you gain control over your mind—empowering you to lead with clarity, creativity, and resilience.

CHAPTER 10
PHYSICAL RESILIENCE

Nutrition and Fitness for Sustained Energy and Endurance

As a founder, you are your business's most valuable asset. The health of your body directly impacts the performance of your mind and your ability to lead effectively. Physical resilience—having the energy, stamina, and overall health to endure the demands of entrepreneurship—is a foundational pillar for success. Without it, even the best ideas and strategies can fall short.

This chapter will focus on how to optimize your physical resilience through nutrition and fitness. By fueling your body with the right nutrients and maintaining a fitness regimen, you'll enhance both your mental sharpness and your capacity to tackle the challenges of business ownership.

The Role of Nutrition in Physical Resilience

The foods you consume have a profound impact on your energy levels, cognitive function, and overall health. What you eat can influence everything from your mood and focus to your decision-making and stress levels. A well-balanced, nutrient-dense diet is key to sustaining energy and maintaining peak performance throughout your day.

Here are some principles for a nutrition plan that supports sustained energy and mental clarity:

1. Prioritize Whole Foods

- Focus on whole, nutrient-dense foods like vegetables, fruits, lean proteins, whole grains, and healthy fats. These foods provide the vitamins, minerals, and antioxidants your body needs to function at its best.
- Avoid processed foods, refined sugars, and excessive caffeine, as these can cause energy crashes, mood swings, and brain fog.

2. Incorporate Healthy Fats

- Omega-3 fatty acids, found in foods like fish, nuts, seeds, and avocados, are critical for brain health and cognitive function. Healthy fats also help to stabilize your energy levels and keep you feeling full longer.
- Coconut oil, olive oil, and grass-fed butter are excellent choices for cooking, as they provide healthy fats that fuel your body throughout the day.

3. Balance Protein and Carbohydrates

- Protein is essential for muscle recovery, immune function, and maintaining energy levels. Include lean protein sources like chicken, turkey, fish, eggs, tofu, and legumes in your meals.
- Carbohydrates, particularly complex carbs found in whole grains, root vegetables, and legumes, provide steady energy for your brain and body. Avoid simple carbs and refined sugars, which can cause spikes and crashes in blood sugar.

4. Hydration is Key

- Staying hydrated is essential for maintaining focus, energy, and physical performance. Dehydration can lead to fatigue, lack of concentration, and irritability. Aim to drink at least 8 cups of water per day, more if you're physically active or consuming caffeine.

5. Meal Timing and Intermittent Fasting

- Intermittent fasting is a dietary strategy where you cycle between periods of eating and fasting. This approach can help regulate insulin levels, increase mental clarity, and promote fat burning. Many founders find intermittent fasting beneficial for sustained energy throughout the day, but it's important to listen to your body and find a meal timing routine that works for you.
- If you're not practicing intermittent fasting, aim to eat smaller, more frequent meals to maintain energy levels. Avoid large, heavy meals that can lead to a post-lunch energy slump.

The Healing Power of Food

We often hear the phrase, "You are what you eat," but what if food was more than just fuel? What if it was medicine? The food we choose to consume has the power to heal or harm, to nourish or neglect. In this chapter, we'll explore how food can serve as medicine for our bodies, offering insights into restoring balance, embracing nature, and understanding the battle against inflammation.

Restoring Balance: Embracing Ourselves as Part of Nature

What Does It Mean to Restore Balance? Restoring balance involves aligning our lives with the natural rhythms of the earth. It requires us to consider how nutrition, activity, work-life harmony, and stress management impact our health. When we stray too far from nature, our bodies remind us through fatigue, illness, and chronic disease.

Key areas to address include:

- Nutrition: Prioritize whole, nutrient-dense foods.
- Microbiome Health: Maintain a balance of beneficial bacteria inside and out.
- Activity Levels: Move often, rest sufficiently.
- Work-Life Balance: Find harmony between responsibilities and relaxation.
- Stress Management: Develop resilience through healthy habits and support systems.

By reconnecting with nature through gardening, hiking, or even simply eating local, seasonal foods, we acknowledge our role as part of the ecosystem. This connection fosters both physical health and mental clarity.

Nutrition: Food as Medicine

Factors Affecting Nutrition

- Rate of Nutrient Consumption: Replace processed foods with whole, unrefined options.
- Nutrient Density: Focus on healthy fats, fiber, vitamins, and clean protein sources.
- Timing: Consider when you eat—intermittent fasting, menstrual cycles, and evening meals all play a role.
- Source: Opt for local, regenerative, and organic produce whenever possible.

- Accessibility: Overcome challenges like food deserts or busy schedules through planning and creativity.

Healing Foods and Their Benefits

- Fats: Grass-fed butter, olive oil, avocados—anti-inflammatory and brain-boosting.
- Fiber: Leafy greens, root vegetables—supports gut health.
- Proteins: Pastured poultry, clean protein powders—repairs tissues and builds strength.
- Aromatics: Herbs like oregano and rosemary—packed with antioxidants.

These foods address specific health concerns, such as:

- Gut Health: Bone broth, root vegetables.
- Mental Health: Healthy fats, colorful fruits and vegetables.
- Skin and Hair: Protein-rich foods, antioxidants.

Foods That Harm: What to Avoid

Not all foods are created equal. Some cause harm by promoting inflammation and oxidative stress.

Common Culprits:

- Fried foods.
- Processed carbohydrates and sugars.
- Non-organic produce laden with pesticides.
- Artificial additives and preservatives.
- Foods high in anti-nutrients, like refined grains.

These foods contribute to chronic conditions such as obesity, cardiovascular disease, and autoimmune disorders. Knowing what to avoid empowers us to make healthier choices.

Understanding Inflammation

What Is Inflammation? Inflammation is the body's natural response to injury or infection. However, chronic inflammation—often caused by poor diet and environmental toxins—leads to oxidative stress, damaging cells, proteins, and DNA.

Sources of Chronic Inflammation:

- Vegetable oils and trans fats.
- Processed sugars.
- Gluten and dairy for those sensitive to them.
- Environmental toxins like glyphosate and pollutants.

Combatting Inflammation:

- Incorporate antioxidant-rich foods, like leafy greens and aromatics.
- Prioritize gut health with probiotics and prebiotics.
- Use natural products for personal care and cleaning to reduce toxin exposure.

Reconnecting With Nature: The Path to Healing

Our biology is rooted in millennia of connection to the earth. From the microorganisms in the soil to the food on our plates, nature sustains us.

Simple Steps to Reconnect:

- Gardening: Cultivate your own produce and herbs.
- Hiking and Foraging: Engage with the natural world.
- Cooking: Prepare meals with whole, local ingredients.
- Support Local Farmers: Build a relationship with your food sources.
- Mindful Practices: Meditate, practice yoga, and foster gratitude for nature's gifts.

By lessening the gap between ourselves and nature, we reclaim vitality and reduce the risk of modern maladies.

Food is more than sustenance—it is medicine. By choosing healing foods, avoiding harmful ones, and fostering a connection with nature, we restore balance and unlock our body's potential for vitality and resilience. Remember, the journey to health begins with a single bite, a single step, a single moment of mindfulness.

Exercise for Physical Resilience

Maintaining a regular fitness routine is just as important as eating well for building physical resilience. Exercise is not only good for your physical health but also improves mood, cognitive function, and mental clarity. Regular physical activity reduces stress, improves sleep, and boosts energy levels—all essential for staying sharp and focused as a founder.

Here are some tips for incorporating fitness into your routine, even when you're pressed for time:

1. Find the Right Type of Exercise for You

- The best exercise routine is one that you enjoy and can maintain consistently. Whether it's strength training, running, yoga, swimming, or cycling, choose activities that align with your interests and lifestyle. Enjoyable activities are more likely to become lasting habits.

2. Strength Training for Endurance and Power

- Strength training, or weightlifting, is essential for building muscle, improving metabolism, and increasing overall stamina. Even just two to three short sessions a week can increase energy levels and improve physical resilience.
- Focus on compound movements like squats, deadlifts, and bench presses, which target multiple muscle groups and increase your overall strength.

3. Cardio for Cardiovascular Health

- Cardiovascular exercise, such as running, cycling, or swimming, improves heart health, boosts circulation, and increases stamina. Cardio also helps to regulate stress hormones like cortisol, which can otherwise interfere with your ability to focus and make decisions.
- Aim for at least 150 minutes of moderate-intensity cardio each week, or 75 minutes of vigorous-intensity cardio, depending on your fitness level.

4. Incorporate Flexibility and Mobility Work

- Flexibility exercises like yoga, Pilates, and stretching are crucial for maintaining mobility and reducing the risk of injury. These activities also promote relaxation and help combat the physical tension that can result from long hours of work and stress.
- Consider adding a yoga session to your weekly routine to enhance flexibility, improve posture, and relieve stress.

5. Make Exercise a Non-Negotiable Habit

- As a busy founder, it's easy to prioritize work over exercise. However, physical resilience is essential for long-term success, and exercise should be treated as a vital part of your routine. Schedule workouts as you would important meetings—block off time in your calendar to ensure consistency.
- Even short, high-intensity workouts (like HIIT) can be effective if you're limited on time. The key is to stay consistent and prioritize your physical health.

The Role of Intermittent Fasting and Autophagy

In recent years, intermittent fasting has become a popular dietary practice, especially among high-performing individuals like founders. Intermittent fasting involves cycling between periods of eating and fasting, and it can have numerous health benefits, including improved brain function, increased energy, and enhanced physical resilience.

One of the key benefits of intermittent fasting is autophagy, a natural process where the body cleans out damaged cells and regenerates new ones. This process can help improve immune function, reduce inflammation, and enhance cognitive function—all critical factors for sustaining the energy and focus needed to grow your business.

Autophagy is typically activated during fasting periods, especially after 12-16 hours without food. While intermittent fasting isn't for everyone, it can be a powerful tool for improving physical and mental resilience when done correctly. If you're new to fasting, it's important to start slowly, listen to your body, and experiment with different fasting windows to find what works best for you.

To illustrate how physical resilience plays a key role in success, here are a few case studies and practical exercises:

Richard Branson's Fitness Routine

Richard Branson, founder of Virgin Group, attributes much of his energy and success to his commitment to physical fitness. Branson has been known to start his day with exercise, often taking a morning swim or bike ride. He credits regular physical activity as the key to maintaining his energy levels and mental clarity. Despite his busy schedule, Branson has made exercise a priority for over 40 years, demonstrating the long-term benefits of maintaining physical resilience.

Arianna Huffington's Shift to Wellness

Arianna Huffington, founder of The Huffington Post, experienced burnout from her relentless work schedule and eventually realized the importance of physical and mental resilience. After collapsing from exhaustion, she began prioritizing sleep, nutrition, and exercise. Huffington now advocates for wellness, emphasizing how taking care of your physical health directly impacts productivity and success. Her story highlights the importance of maintaining a healthy body to sustain your energy and focus.

The 10-Minute Morning Movement Routine

To kickstart your day with physical resilience, try this quick morning workout routine:

- 2 minutes: Jumping jacks
- 3 minutes: Bodyweight squats
- 2 minutes: Push-ups (modified if needed)

- 2 minutes: Plank hold
- 1 minute: Stretching

This short routine is designed to increase blood flow, energize your body, and set a positive tone for the rest of your day. Perform this routine in the morning before you dive into your work, and notice the boost in energy and mental clarity it provides.

The Hydration Challenge

Challenge yourself to drink at least 8 cups of water a day for one week. Track your hydration and note any improvements in your energy levels, focus, and mood. Hydration is a simple but powerful way to enhance physical resilience and ensure your body and mind are functioning at their best.

Physical resilience is crucial for maintaining the energy, focus, and stamina needed to grow a successful business. Through proper nutrition, regular exercise, and strategies like intermittent fasting, you can optimize your physical health and build the endurance necessary to keep pace with the demands of entrepreneurship.

CHAPTER 11
SPIRITUAL RESILIENCE

Aligning Your Business with Your Personal Values and Purpose

In the world of business, especially when navigating the complexities and challenges of entrepreneurship, spiritual resilience is often overlooked. However, it is one of the most powerful forms of resilience a founder can cultivate. Spiritual resilience is about staying grounded, maintaining a sense of purpose, and aligning your business with your core values. It allows you to navigate the highs and lows of entrepreneurship with an inner sense of direction and meaning.

When you lead with purpose and are aligned with your values, it not only enhances your own personal resilience but also helps foster a more authentic, values-driven business. This chapter explores how spiritual resilience is a key component of your overall well-being as a founder, offering both the emotional fortitude and clarity needed to lead with confidence and vision.

Why Spiritual Resilience Matters for Founders

Spiritual resilience is the ability to stay true to your inner self and purpose, even when external pressures mount. In a fast-paced, results-driven world, it's easy to lose sight of why you started your business in the first place. The pursuit of profits, market share, or growth can sometimes overshadow the core mission that brought you into entrepreneurship. This is where spiritual resilience plays a pivotal role.

Founders who are spiritually resilient have a deep understanding of their why—the personal values, beliefs, and passions that motivate them. They lead with a sense of purpose that transcends short-term wins, and in doing so, they create businesses that are not only financially successful but also meaningful and fulfilling.

Spiritual resilience is what allows you to:

- Stay focused on your long-term vision
- Stay grounded when faced with challenges
- Make decisions aligned with your core values
- Inspire your team and customers with authentic leadership

The Power of Mindfulness and Meditation in Decision-Making

In today's fast-paced business world, the ability to make clear, thoughtful decisions is crucial. Mindfulness and meditation are powerful practices that can support founders in cultivating this mental clarity. By practicing mindfulness, you cultivate the ability to be fully present in the moment, which helps reduce stress and enhances your decision-making process.

What is Mindfulness?

Mindfulness is the practice of paying attention to the present moment, without judgment. It involves observing your thoughts, feelings, and bodily sensations as they arise, while maintaining a calm and open attitude. When you practice mindfulness, you train your mind to detach from distractions, allowing you to focus on what's truly important.

For founders, mindfulness can help:

- Reduce stress: By focusing on the present, you reduce feelings of overwhelm and anxiety.
- Enhance emotional regulation: Mindfulness helps you become more aware of your emotional responses, allowing you to respond thoughtfully rather than react impulsively.
- Improve focus and clarity: By clearing away mental clutter, mindfulness enables you to make decisions with greater clarity and intentionality.

How Meditation Supports Spiritual Resilience

Meditation is a tool that helps you develop mindfulness. It is a practice that allows you to create mental space, quiet the mind, and connect with your inner self. Regular meditation helps you cultivate the spiritual resilience needed to stay calm under pressure, tap into your intuition, and maintain your sense of purpose.

Studies have shown that meditation can:

- Boost emotional intelligence: Meditation increases self-awareness and empathy, which enhances your ability to lead with compassion and authenticity.

- Improve decision-making: By quieting the mind, meditation allows you to make decisions based on a deep sense of clarity and inner guidance.
- Reduce stress: Meditation lowers cortisol levels, the body's stress hormone, helping you stay calm and composed during high-stakes situations.

A simple meditation practice, such as focusing on your breath for just 5-10 minutes a day, can make a significant difference in your overall well-being and spiritual resilience.

Overcoming Obstacles with Spiritual Practices

The entrepreneurial journey is filled with obstacles, setbacks, and unexpected challenges. What differentiates successful founders from others is not just their ability to overcome these obstacles, but their ability to stay aligned with their purpose throughout the process. This is where spiritual practices come into play.

Spiritual practices—such as prayer, meditation, yoga, or journaling—help founders stay connected to their inner strength, even in the face of adversity. These practices provide a grounding force that can help you navigate difficult decisions, maintain your sense of calm, and stay true to your values.

Here are some spiritual practices that can support you in building resilience:

1. Gratitude Journaling

- Taking a few minutes each day to write down things you're grateful for can help shift your mindset from one of scarcity to abundance. It allows you to focus on the positives in your life and business, even when things feel challenging.

- Research shows that gratitude practices can increase happiness, reduce stress, and improve overall well-being. For founders, a gratitude practice is an essential tool for staying optimistic and resilient.

2. Visualization of Purpose

- Spend time each day visualizing your business success, but more importantly, visualize how that success aligns with your greater sense of purpose. How does your work serve the world? How does it align with your values? This connection to a higher purpose can help you stay motivated, even when facing setbacks.

- Visualization of your purpose will help you focus on the why of your business, rather than getting lost in the how. When you align with your mission, your obstacles become stepping stones rather than roadblocks.

3. Prayer or Affirmations

- If you have a spiritual or religious practice, prayer can be an incredibly powerful tool for maintaining spiritual resilience. Whether you pray for guidance, strength, or clarity, prayer can connect you with your inner wisdom and provide peace of mind.

- If prayer is not part of your practice, affirmations can serve a similar purpose. Affirmations are positive statements that help you stay focused on your purpose and capabilities. For example: "I am aligned with my purpose and trust that every challenge is an opportunity for growth."

4. Yoga and Movement Practices

- Yoga and other forms of conscious movement allow you to connect your body and mind. They help release

tension, increase awareness, and bring balance to your life. Yoga can also be a form of meditation, helping you center your thoughts and focus on the present moment.
- Engaging in physical activity that incorporates mindfulness—like yoga or Tai Chi—can support your spiritual resilience by grounding you in the present moment and strengthening your connection to your inner self.

Howard Schultz and the Purpose-Driven Business

Howard Schultz, the former CEO of Starbucks, transformed the coffee company from a local business into a global powerhouse by connecting his personal values to the company's mission. Schultz believed that business could be a force for good, and he was committed to building a company that treated its employees and customers with dignity and respect. By aligning the company's goals with his own sense of purpose, Schultz built a brand that inspired loyalty, not just because of its products but because of its values.

Chapter 7: Spiritual Resilience – The Inner Path to Healing and Wholeness

Founders are often lauded for their grit, vision, and drive—but rarely is enough attention given to their spiritual foundation. Yet, it is often the unseen inner landscape that determines how well we navigate the storms of business and life. Spiritual resilience is the ability to remain grounded, clear, and connected to purpose in the face of adversity. It's not about religion; it's about alignment, authenticity, and awareness.

To build spiritual resilience, we must confront what stands in the way of our healing and growth. Let's explore the inner terrain—beginning with the roadblocks.

Roadblocks to Healing: Understanding the Inner Terrain

Physiology: The Foundation of Stress Responses

Our bodies are our first responders to stress and trauma. Through mechanisms like the "fight, flight, or freeze" response, our physiology works to protect us. But when those systems are chronically activated or thrown out of balance, they become obstacles instead of assets.

- **Chronic Activation of the Stress Response**: When stress hormones like cortisol remain elevated due to constant activation of the HPA axis, we experience immune suppression, chronic inflammation, and disrupted sleep. This persistent alert state prevents the nervous system from feeling safe enough to begin healing.

- **Autonomic Nervous System Dysregulation**: Trauma often shifts us into sympathetic overdrive, leaving the parasympathetic "rest and digest" functions underactive. This imbalance causes sleep disturbances, gut dysfunction, and emotional reactivity.

- **Neuroplasticity Impairment**: Long-term trauma changes the brain's architecture, inhibiting our ability to learn, adapt, and rewire old patterns.

- **Inflammation and Brain Function**: Chronic inflammation hinders neurotransmitter function and impairs emotional regulation, creating a cycle where trauma symptoms persist and deepen.

Nutrition: Fueling Recovery from the Inside Out

Trauma-informed healing begins with nourishment. Food is more than fuel—it's a biochemical signal that influences every system in the body.

- **Brain Health & Mood**: Nutrients like omega-3s, magnesium, and B-vitamins support neurotransmitters like serotonin and dopamine. Deficiencies contribute to anxiety, brain fog, and fatigue.
- **The Gut-Brain Axis**: Over 90% of serotonin is produced in the gut. A poor diet disrupts gut flora, leading to mood swings and increased emotional reactivity.
- **Blood Sugar & Emotional Stability**: Refined carbs spike and crash blood sugar, destabilizing mood and energy. Stabilizing your nutrition stabilizes your nervous system.

Self-Awareness as a Spiritual Practice

Self-awareness is where healing begins. When we can distinguish between the Core Self, the Ego, and the Body, we can begin to break free from trauma loops and return to our center.

- **Core Self**: Your unchanging essence—wise, whole, and capable.
- **Ego**: A survival strategy shaped by trauma, fear, and societal expectations. It seeks control, validation, and safety.
- **Body**: The physical vessel that carries trauma, but also carries the ability to release it.

Through self-inquiry, meditation, and reflection, we can:

- Recognize how egoic patterns block healing.
- Reclaim our true nature beyond trauma.
- Initiate holistic healing through integration of mind, body, and spirit.

Breaking Through Cognitive Stuck Points

Borrowed from Cognitive Processing Therapy, "stuck points" are trauma-rooted beliefs that prevent us from moving forward:

- "I deserved what happened."
- "I can never trust again."
- "The world is dangerous."

These aren't facts. They're narratives—and they can be changed. Identify the stuck point. Challenge it. Reframe it. And integrate a new, life-giving belief.

Diagnosis Is Not Destiny

Getting ac PTSD diagnosis can feel both like a relief and a life sentence. It offers clarity, but it can also become a box. Don't confuse description with identity.

- **Diagnosis helps direct treatment.**
- **But over-identifying with it can reinforce limitation.**

You are not broken. You are healing. Let the diagnosis be a doorway, not a destination.

The Stoic Path to Inner Liberation

The Stoic philosophers offer timeless wisdom for letting go of the past and reclaiming the present. For founders navigating personal pain while building the future, Stoicism offers spiritual armor.

- **Focus on What You Control**: You cannot change the past, but you can change your perception of it.

- **Shift Your Judgments**: It's not the trauma, but your meaning-making around it, that creates suffering.
- **Practice Negative Visualization**: Imagine worse outcomes—not to invite fear, but to cultivate gratitude for what is.
- **Build Your Inner Citadel**: Fortify your mind against life's chaos by cultivating calm, courage, and clarity.
- **Forgive and Accept**: Acceptance is not approval—it's surrendering the illusion of control. Forgiveness clears space for your healing.

Growth After Trauma: From Wound to Wisdom

The most resilient founders don't just bounce back—they transform. Trauma becomes a teacher.

- **Redefine What Happened**: Pain isn't your identity—it's part of your story.
- **Embrace Vulnerability**: Sharing and seeking help takes courage. It opens the door to connection and freedom.
- **Challenge Shame**: Your worth is not up for debate. You are not what happened to you.
- **Explore Therapy**: Rewiring beliefs takes time and tools. Therapy helps you shift from reaction to reflection.
- **Experiment and Evolve**: Try new experiences, explore different environments. Expand your identity beyond the past.
- **Be Open to the Long Game**: Healing is not linear. Be gentle with yourself as you grow.

Task and Purpose: The Spiritual Fuel for Founders

When healing feels daunting, purpose provides a North Star.

- **Purpose Provides Direction**: It keeps you focused on what matters and away from spirals of rumination.
- **Purpose Connects You to Others**: Whether it's your team or your tribe, shared mission creates belonging.
- **Purpose Builds Resilience**: When setbacks come (and they will), purpose keeps you moving forward.
- **Purpose Transcends Pain**: Even suffering becomes meaningful when it shapes your impact.

Take time to map your purpose. Ask yourself:

- What does my business stand for?
- What legacy am I building?
- How does my company reflect my personal values?

Practices That Cultivate Spiritual Resilience

- **Mindfulness**: Begin each day with 5–10 minutes of focused breath. Set an intention. Anchor in presence.
- **Journaling**: Reflect on growth, gratitude, and patterns. Name what you're releasing and what you're becoming.
- **Community**: Share your story. Be witnessed. Healing happens in connection.
- **Visualization**: See yourself as healed. Whole. On purpose. Practice the future you desire.

Spiritual resilience is not abstract. It's practical. It's personal. It's powerful.

As you build your business, don't neglect the one who's building it—you. Anchor yourself in meaning, align your actions with purpose, and trust that the version of you on the other side of healing is wiser, stronger, and ready to lead with heart.

Your spirit is not a side note to your success. It is the source of it.

CHAPTER 12
ENVIRONMENTAL RESILIENCE

Optimizing Your Physical and Social Environment for Growth

As a founder, the environment in which you work and live plays a crucial role in your personal well-being, productivity, and ultimately, the success of your business. Whether it's the physical space you occupy, the social networks you cultivate, or the culture you build within your organization, environmental resilience is about creating surroundings that support your mental, emotional, and physical health, as well as your business goals.

Environmental resilience goes beyond the physical aspects of your workspace or home. It also encompasses the relationships you foster, the energy of the spaces you inhabit, and the overall atmosphere you create around yourself. This chapter delves into how you can optimize both your physical and social environments to support your resilience as a founder.

Why Environmental Resilience Matters for Founders

The spaces you inhabit—whether your office, home, or even the city you live in—have a profound impact on your well-being. If your environment is chaotic, cluttered, or toxic, it can drain your energy, hinder your focus, and increase stress. On the other hand, a well-designed, harmonious environment can inspire creativity, improve mental clarity, and foster positive relationships.

As a founder, you need a space that not only supports your work but nurtures your health, helps you stay connected to your purpose, and encourages collaboration and innovation. This is where environmental resilience comes into play. By consciously designing your environment, both physical and social, you can enhance your ability to navigate challenges, manage stress, and stay focused on your long-term vision.

Understanding Stress as a Spiritual Signal

In the journey of building a purpose-driven life, stress is often miscast as the villain—an unwanted guest disrupting peace, productivity, and progress. But what if we reframed stress not as an obstacle, but as a spiritual messenger? A divine nudge calling us to pay attention, evolve, and realign.

Stress is not just a mental or physical experience; it's a deeply spiritual one. It arises when something in our external environment clashes with our internal expectations, desires, or identity. When this happens, the body responds with the well-known "fight, flight, or freeze" mechanism. While this ancient survival response once saved us from predators, in the modern world, it often becomes chronically activated—especially for founders navigating pressure, uncertainty, and high stakes.

Why Understanding Stress Is Foundational to Spiritual Growth

To lead others, we must first lead ourselves. And that begins with knowing how our internal systems respond to the world around us. Understanding stress is essential for:

- **Self-awareness:** Recognizing stress patterns empowers us to respond instead of react.
- **Health preservation:** Chronic stress leads to disease, fatigue, and burnout—disrupting our divine mission.
- **Wise decision-making:** A calm nervous system allows for clarity, discernment, and higher thinking.
- **Connected relationships:** Unmanaged stress can harm the very connections that sustain our purpose.
- **Spiritual alignment:** Stress can reveal misalignments between our values and our actions.

The Inner Dialogue: Cognitive Activation Theory of Stress (CATS)

According to the Cognitive Activation Theory of Stress (CATS), stress is not just about what's happening—it's about how we interpret it. This makes stress a conversation between our environment and our beliefs.

1. **Cognitive Appraisal:** We evaluate whether an event is threatening or manageable based on our perceptions.
2. **Expectancy:** If we believe we can handle it, we're more likely to transform stress into strength.

3. **Physiological Activation:** Our thoughts trigger the body's response—faster heartbeat, muscle tension, adrenaline.
4. **Coping Response:** How we choose to act determines whether stress leads to growth or suffering.
5. **Spiritual Insight:** Every moment of stress invites us to ask, "What is this trying to teach me?"

The Power of Belief: Expectancy as a Spiritual Practice

Our expectations shape our reality. Two founders enter a pitch meeting:

- One believes they're prepared and worthy of success. Their stress energizes them.
- The other doubts their ability. The same situation becomes a source of anxiety.

What changes everything? Belief. Expectancy is the foundation of faith—the conviction that we are capable, supported, and guided. It allows stress to become fuel instead of friction.

Stress Isn't the Enemy—Avoiding It Is

Stress exists on a spectrum. It's not about eliminating stress, but learning to alchemize it.

- **Eustress (Good Stress):** Fuels motivation, creativity, and performance.
- **Distress (Bad Stress):** Overwhelms, isolates, and burns us out.

Your spiritual task is to cultivate the wisdom to know the difference and the practices to stay centered.

Coping as Sacred Strategy

Stress invites us into choice. Will we move toward growth or retreat into avoidance?

- **Problem-Focused Coping:** When the situation can be changed, take action.
- **Emotion-Focused Coping:** When the situation cannot be changed, tend to your inner world.

Within these, we also choose between:

- **Active Coping:** Journaling, talking to a coach, seeking clarity, taking responsibility.
- **Passive Coping:** Numbing, procrastinating, blaming, or disconnecting from our spirit.

Choose your tools like a spiritual warrior. This is not self-help—it's soul stewardship.

Daily Practices to Transmute Stress

1. **Awareness:** Track your triggers. Where in your life do you feel chronically activated?
2. **Breathwork & Meditation:** Regulate your nervous system and create space for divine insight.
3. **Movement:** Use exercise, walking, or yoga to transmute energy.
4. **Community:** Talk it out. Let trusted relationships hold space for you.
5. **Reframing:** Ask, "What lesson is hidden in this? What is this trying to awaken in me?"
6. **Spiritual Boundaries:** Say no to what's misaligned. Protect your time, energy, and spirit.

Stress as a Spiritual Compass

Stress shows us where we are out of alignment—either with our environment or with ourselves. It asks us to pause, reflect, and recalibrate.

The next time you feel stress, don't suppress it. Invite it in like a messenger. Ask:

- What's misaligned here?
- What needs to be expressed, healed, or released?
- How can I return to the present moment?

Your ability to work with stress—not against it—is one of the most profound spiritual skills you can cultivate.

In this way, stress becomes sacred. A guidepost. A call back to the center. A reminder that you are not here to be crushed by life's challenges, but to rise through them—resilient, conscious, and connected to something greater than yourself.

Self-Awareness

Begin by cultivating self-awareness to identify your individual stressors, triggers, and reactions. Reflect on past experiences and observe your thoughts, emotions, and behaviors in response to stress. Developing self-awareness allows you to recognize patterns and implement tailored strategies to cope effectively.

Experimentation

Experiment with different coping mechanisms to determine which strategies work best for you in specific situations. Try a variety of techniques such as:

- Relaxation exercises: Deep breathing, meditation, or progressive muscle relaxation.
- Journaling: Writing down thoughts and feelings to gain clarity.
- Physical activity: Exercise as a way to release tension and boost endorphins.
- Social support: Talking to trusted friends, family, or professionals for advice and encouragement.

Mindfulness

Practice mindfulness to stay present and observe your thoughts and feelings without judgment. Mindfulness techniques can help you develop greater self-awareness, emotional regulation, and resilience in managing stress. Consider methods like:

- Guided meditation
- Mindful breathing exercises
- Yoga or tai chi

Seeking Support

Don't hesitate to seek support from trusted individuals or mental health professionals. Sharing your stressors and receiving validation can provide new perspectives and encouragement. Building strong support systems fosters a sense of security and reduces isolation.

The Power of Eight Minutes

Entrepreneurship is an endurance sport, and resilience is not just about inner fortitude—it's also about shaping an environment that sustains and strengthens you. One of the most overlooked aspects of resilience is how we navigate support and space within our personal and professional ecosystems. The way we frame our needs and communicate them can determine whether we feel trapped in a cycle of stress or empowered by our surroundings.

A simple but powerful concept that speaks to this balance is Simon Sinek's approach to meaningful connection. He often asks, *"Do you have eight minutes?"*—a way of signaling to a friend or colleague that you need a focused moment of their time. This phrase allows both people to set expectations and engage in a real, uninterrupted exchange.

But what about when the need isn't for connection, but for space?

"Can You Give Me Eight Minutes?"—Creating Space to Reset

Just as founders need support, they also need room to breathe. The cognitive demands of entrepreneurship—decision fatigue, high-stakes problem-solving, and emotional turbulence—can overwhelm even the most resilient leaders. When external pressures escalate, a founder's environment can either suffocate them further or provide a structured way to reset.

This is where a simple shift in language can be transformational:

Instead of "Do you have eight minutes?" to invite connection, consider *"Can you give me eight minutes?"* to request space.

This phrase accomplishes two things:

1. It gives permission to pause – Entrepreneurs often feel obligated to push through stress, but a structured break signals that recalibration is not only allowed but essential.
2. It sets a boundary with clarity – Instead of vanishing for an undefined period or spiraling into avoidance, this communicates a temporary disengagement that others can respect.

The Science of the Eight-Minute Reset

Why eight minutes? While the number itself is symbolic, research on stress recovery and cognitive load suggests that micro-breaks—anywhere from 5 to 15 minutes—can dramatically reduce cortisol levels, restore executive function, and improve emotional regulation.

In practice, this might look like:

- Stepping away from a high-stress meeting before reacting impulsively.
- Taking a brief, structured walk to regain perspective.
- Using breathwork, meditation, or simple visualization techniques to reset.
- Giving yourself permission to disengage from stimuli (emails, Slack, phone calls) to re-enter with clarity.

Embedding This in Founder Culture

Imagine a work environment where founders and teams normalize both support and space:

- Before a tough conversation: *"Do you have eight minutes?"*

- Before burnout sets in: *"Can you give me eight minutes?"*

By integrating this language into daily interactions, founders can design environments that foster resilience rather than drain it. This is not about weakness—it's about mastering energy management, ensuring that when a founder is present, they are truly present, and when they need space, they can take it with intention.

In the long game of entrepreneurship, those who balance connection and recalibration are the ones who endure, adapt, and thrive.

Adaptability

Be flexible and adaptable in your coping strategies, as different stressors may require different approaches. Develop a versatile toolkit of coping mechanisms to draw upon based on the nature and intensity of the stressor. Adapting your strategies ensures that you remain resilient in the face of varying challenges.

By actively engaging in these strategies, individuals can manage stress and build resilience, fostering a proactive approach to life's challenges. This empowers individuals to overcome automatic, subconscious responses to stress and cultivate a sense of agency and hope.

When Coping Mechanisms Are Absent

Without effective coping mechanisms, individuals may experience a sense of diminished agency, self-worth, and self-efficacy. This can lead to feelings of learned helplessness or hopelessness, which can exacerbate stress and undermine mental health.

Learned Helplessness vs. Learned Hopelessness

- Learned Helplessness: Occurs when individuals perceive they have no control over stressors, leading to a sense of resignation and passivity. This often results from repeated exposure to uncontrollable situations, eroding confidence and action.
- Learned Hopelessness: Extends beyond helplessness, involving a pervasive belief that efforts to improve circumstances will always fail. This mindset can lead to despair, apathy, and disengagement, contributing to depression and a loss of motivation.

Allostatic Load and Stress Adaptation

Understanding Allostasis

Allostasis refers to the body's ability to maintain stability through physiological and behavioral changes in response to stressors. Unlike homeostasis, which aims to keep conditions constant, allostasis allows for dynamic adjustments to meet changing demands.

Key Aspects:

1. Dynamic Adaptation: Adjustments in hormone levels, neural activity, and cardiovascular function to meet specific challenges.
2. Flexibility: Emphasizes adaptability over maintaining fixed physiological set points.
3. Energy Efficiency: Minimizes energy expenditure while achieving stability.
4. Anticipation: Prepares for future challenges based on prior experiences.

Example of Allostasis

Imagine encountering a sudden physical threat, such as being chased by a grizzly bear. The body activates the fight-or-flight response, releasing adrenaline and cortisol, increasing heart rate and blood pressure, and enhancing alertness. Once the threat passes, the body gradually returns to a baseline state, demonstrating adaptability and resilience.

Allostatic Load

Chronic stress can lead to an increased allostatic load, the cumulative wear and tear on the body. Prolonged stress responses can contribute to:

- Cardiovascular issues
- Immune dysfunction
- Mental health challenges like anxiety or depression

Stress Adaptation Techniques

Stress adaptation involves physiological and psychological adjustments to cope with stressors effectively. Here are examples:

Exposure Therapy

Exposure therapy helps individuals confront and adapt to feared stimuli systematically. Examples include:

- Specific Phobias (e.g., Fear of Flying): Gradual exposure, from imagining flying to taking short flights, reduces fear and physiological responses over time.
- PTSD (Trauma Reminders): Controlled exposure to trauma-related stimuli helps reprocess memories and reduce distress.

- Social Anxiety (Public Speaking): Progressive exposure, from small groups to larger audiences, builds confidence and reduces anxiety.

Cold Therapy

Ice baths involve controlled exposure to cold stressors. Gradual immersion reduces the physiological stress response over time, enhancing resilience and promoting both physical and mental benefits.

Exercise Training

Structured physical activity challenges the body, promoting both physiological and psychological adaptation. Benefits include improved cardiovascular efficiency, increased resilience, and enhanced mental well-being.

Social Determinants of Stress Resilience

Social factors significantly influence how individuals perceive and cope with stress.

Key Factors:

1. Social Support: Strong networks provide emotional and practical assistance.
2. Socioeconomic Status (SES): Access to resources like healthcare and education mitigates stress.
3. Community Resources: Support groups and community organizations foster resilience.
4. Cultural Factors: Cultural practices and norms shape coping strategies and resilience.
5. Social Connectedness: Meaningful interactions and relationships enhance belonging and reduce stress.

6. Social Capital: High social capital, with trust and reciprocity, promotes collective resilience.
7. Workplace Support: Positive relationships and supportive environments reduce work-related stress.

By addressing social determinants and fostering supportive communities, individuals can enhance their resilience and improve overall well-being.

The Impact of Your Physical Environment

The physical environment plays a significant role in determining how effectively you can work and how you feel on a daily basis. Your workspace, the design of your office or home, and the quality of your surroundings can either support or hinder your productivity, creativity, and overall well-being.

1. Decluttering for Mental Clarity

A cluttered space often leads to a cluttered mind. When your workspace is disorganized, it can be challenging to focus, prioritize, or even think clearly. Studies have shown that physical clutter increases stress levels and impairs cognitive function, making it harder to make decisions or complete tasks.

Actionable Steps:

- Declutter your workspace: Start by removing unnecessary items that don't add value or that distract you from your goals. Keep only the essentials within reach—those things that inspire you and help you focus.
- Implement the "one in, one out" rule: This simple approach ensures that every new item you bring into your

space serves a purpose, while you let go of things that no longer align with your work or goals.

2. Design Your Space for Focus and Creativity

Your environment can also affect how you feel while you're working. For example, lighting, colors, furniture, and even noise levels all impact your ability to concentrate and engage in creative thinking.

Actionable Steps:

- Use natural light: Natural light boosts mood and energy levels. If possible, position your desk near a window to take advantage of daylight. If that's not feasible, consider using full-spectrum light bulbs to mimic natural light.
- Incorporate plants: Studies show that indoor plants can reduce stress, improve air quality, and increase productivity. Adding greenery to your office can help you feel more grounded and energized.
- Create dedicated spaces: If you work from home or in a flexible office, designate specific areas for different tasks. A space for deep focus, a space for creative brainstorming, and a space for meetings can all help you maintain clear boundaries between work modes.

3. Managing Noise and Distractions

Noise is one of the most significant disruptors of focus. Whether it's background chatter, music, or even the hum of electronic devices, noise can interfere with your ability to concentrate, think clearly, and maintain your energy levels.

Actionable Steps:

- Control your environment: If you're in a noisy environment, use noise-canceling headphones or play ambient sounds that promote concentration (e.g., white noise or nature sounds).

- Create sound boundaries: Set clear boundaries with colleagues, family members, or anyone sharing your workspace. Communicate when you need focused time and when you're available for collaboration.

Chapter X: The Spiritual Foundations of Connection and Attachment

For founders, relationships are the currency of success—and the source of some of the greatest stress. Whether you're navigating dynamics with co-founders, investors, team members, or loved ones, your ability to connect authentically and communicate clearly is essential. But often, the patterns that guide our relationships aren't conscious decisions—they're rooted deep in our nervous system.

This is where attachment theory comes in. Originating from the work of John Bowlby, attachment theory explains how early interactions with caregivers shape how we relate to others for the rest of our lives. These foundational patterns—secure, avoidant, anxious, and disorganized—don't just influence romantic relationships. They quietly guide how we respond to conflict, build trust, lead teams, and handle stress.

Understanding your attachment style is not about labeling yourself—it's about building self-awareness and, ultimately, spiritual and emotional freedom. When you understand why you react the way you do in relationships, you can choose how to show up instead of being run by unconscious patterns.

Attachment Styles and the Founder's Journey

Secure Attachment: You're comfortable with intimacy, trust, and interdependence. You lead with calm confidence and build stable relationships.

Avoidant Attachment: You prefer independence, may feel discomfort with emotional closeness, and can come off as aloof or overly self-reliant.

Anxious Attachment: You crave closeness but fear rejection, often seeking reassurance and becoming preoccupied with others' responses.

Disorganized Attachment: A blend of both avoidant and anxious patterns, often rooted in trauma. You may alternate between closeness and withdrawal, creating confusion in relationships.

As a founder, your attachment style affects everything from how you handle conflict with a co-founder to how you manage a team, pitch to investors, or balance personal relationships with your mission. Here's how it plays out in key areas:

Co-Founder Relationships

- **Secure founders** create strong communication loops and navigate disagreement with curiosity and mutual respect.
- **Avoidant founders** may resist emotional conversations or delay difficult discussions.
- **Anxious founders** might feel overly responsible for harmony and seek constant validation.
- **Disorganized founders** may create instability by oscillating between engagement and avoidance.

Team and Culture

Your leadership style sets the tone for your company's emotional culture:

- **Secure leaders** foster psychological safety and stability.
- **Avoidant leaders** might focus only on performance, neglecting relational connection.
- **Anxious leaders** may micromanage or struggle with delegation.
- **Disorganized leaders** might seem unpredictable or reactive, eroding trust.

Investors and Stakeholders

In high-stakes conversations with investors or partners:

- **Secure attachment** helps you show up confidently and communicate clearly.
- **Avoidant styles** may avoid vulnerability, which can undermine transparency.
- **Anxious tendencies** might lead to over-explaining or people-pleasing.
- **Disorganized patterns** can create inconsistency, leading to questions about leadership reliability.

Personal Relationships

Outside the business, your attachment style impacts:

- How you handle stress and lean on (or avoid) support.
- The depth of your connections and sense of belonging.
- Your ability to recharge, reflect, and stay spiritually grounded.

Shifting Toward Secure Attachment

Attachment styles are adaptive—not fixed. With awareness and practice, you can shift toward more secure, grounded ways of relating. Here are tools for transformation:

1. Self-Awareness Practices

- Journal about moments of conflict or emotional charge—what was triggered?
- Identify recurring patterns in how you relate to others.
- Practice mindfulness to observe without judgment.

2. Conscious Relationships

- Seek mentors, coaches, or partners with secure traits.
- Practice healthy vulnerability—share your inner world gradually.
- Build interdependence, not codependence.

3. Emotional Regulation

- Use breathwork, somatic practices, and grounding techniques to manage emotional overwhelm.
- Reflect instead of react—especially under stress.

4. Therapeutic Tools

- Explore modalities like Internal Family Systems (IFS), Emotionally Focused Therapy (EFT), or somatic-based therapy.
- Identify and reframe core beliefs around trust, safety, and worthiness.

Applying Attachment Awareness to Your Business

Create a Culture of Psychological Safety

- Normalize emotional intelligence and open dialogue.
- Celebrate feedback and continuous learning.

Foster Relational Resilience

- Invest in team bonding, shared purpose, and trust-building rituals.
- Encourage honesty and repair after conflict—not avoidance.

Model Secure Leadership

- Show consistency, transparency, and grounded decision-making.
- Acknowledge mistakes without shame—model growth.

Real-World Examples

- **The Avoidant Leader:** After years of avoiding tough conversations, a founder began therapy and committed to weekly check-ins with their team. Morale and retention soared.
- **The Anxious Negotiator:** With coaching and breathwork, a founder learned to self-regulate before investor calls, replacing anxiety with grounded confidence.
- **The Disorganized Innovator:** Through structured routines and internal work, a visionary leader turned emotional unpredictability into consistent, inspired leadership.

The Power of Social Environments

Your relationships either drain or sustain you. Cultivating a support system and a conscious work culture is essential to staying resilient and spiritually connected.

1. Build a Supportive Circle

- Surround yourself with mentors, peers, and friends who reflect back your potential.
- Join or create founder peer groups for shared reflection and accountability.

2. Lead a Resilient Culture

- Model healthy boundaries, celebrate progress, and foster purpose-driven work.
- Prioritize emotional health as much as performance.

3. Protect Your Energy

- Say no to what drains you. Say yes to what aligns.
- Schedule time for stillness, solitude, and restoration.

Your attachment style isn't a limitation—it's a map. It reveals where healing is needed and where growth is possible. As a founder, when you do the inner work to shift your relational patterns, you don't just build better companies. You build a more grounded, connected, and spiritually aligned life.

Leadership begins within.

Chapter 10: The Foundation of Healthy Boundaries

As a founder, your energy is one of your most valuable resources. How you protect it—through the boundaries you set—determines your capacity to lead, relate, and recover. Boundaries are not walls. They are bridges of understanding that define what's acceptable in your life and what is not. They protect your time, energy, focus, and emotional well-being so you can show up with purpose, not resentment.

Defining Boundaries

Boundaries are the internal rules we establish to protect our mental, emotional, physical, and even spiritual health. They are the invisible lines that determine how we interact with others, what we accept from them, and how we respond. Without boundaries, burnout is inevitable. With them, balance and resilience become possible.

Why Boundaries Are Essential for Founders

- **Preserve Mental Health**: Boundaries help prevent over-commitment, decision fatigue, and emotional depletion.
- **Enhance Focus and Productivity**: Clear boundaries protect your schedule and priorities, allowing for deep work and strategic thinking.
- **Build Self-Worth**: Saying "no" is an act of self-respect. It signals that your time and well-being are just as important as any external demand.

Six Types of Boundaries (and How to Use Them)

1. **Physical Boundaries**
   - Respect for personal space and physical needs.
   - *Founder Tip*: Schedule non-negotiable breaks to recharge.

2. **Emotional Boundaries**
   - Guard your emotional energy and choose when to engage.
   - *Founder Tip*: Don't entertain draining conversations before key meetings or pitches.

3. **Time Boundaries**
   - Protect your calendar and delegate distractions.
   - *Founder Tip*: Implement "deep work" blocks where no one can interrupt you.

4. **Sexual Boundaries**
   - Essential in both personal and professional spaces.
   - *Founder Tip*: Create clear policies on professional conduct to prevent discomfort or violations.

5. **Intellectual Boundaries**
   - Respect for ideas, beliefs, and discussions.
   - *Founder Tip*: Foster constructive debates without personal attacks.

6. **Material Boundaries**
   - Clarity around lending money, sharing tools, or using shared assets.

- *Founder Tip*: Set access rules for company resources and tools.

Recognizing Boundary Violations

- You feel drained after conversations.
- You're resentful but haven't said anything.
- You regularly deprioritize yourself to please others.

Consequences of Weak Boundaries

- Emotional burnout and mental fatigue.
- Relationship conflict due to misaligned expectations.
- Diminished productivity and constant reactivity.

Strategies to Set and Maintain Boundaries

- **Communicate Clearly**: Use "I" statements and be direct but respectful.
- **Practice Self-Awareness**: Tune in to your needs and adjust boundaries accordingly.
- **Learn to Say No**: Without guilt. Protecting your purpose is worth it.
- **Be Consistent**: Reinforce your limits with actions, not just words.

Supporting Others Without Losing Yourself

Boundaries also enhance your ability to support others. Founders who know where they end and others begin are better at mentoring, leading, and growing strong teams.

Ways to Offer Support with Boundaries

- **Active Listening**: Create space without fixing.
- **Emotional Labeling**: Name the emotion to normalize it.
- **Mentorship**: Share experience, not control.
- **Connection**: Share opportunities, introductions, and insights without overextending.

Boundaries in Action: Founder Mode vs. Manager Mode

In **Founder Mode**, you are the emotional engine behind the vision. You're deeply invested—not just in the company's mission, but in the people bringing it to life. This emotional investment is often a superpower, fueling creativity and authentic connection. However, it also comes with challenges. Founders in this mode frequently struggle with delegation because their identity is intertwined with the business. It's easy to over-identify with outcomes, internalize team struggles, and absorb emotional labor far beyond what's sustainable. To thrive in this mode, founders need to set boundaries that protect their energy, prevent emotional exhaustion, and allow them to lead without losing themselves.

In **Manager Mode**, the focus shifts from vision to execution. This role relies more heavily on systems, structures, and accountability. It's generally easier in this mode to implement and maintain boundaries through established protocols—like defined working hours, communication policies, or standard operating procedures. But there's a tradeoff: it can become overly mechanical. Leaders in this mode must be mindful not to become rigid or emotionally disconnected. True leadership means knowing how to apply structure without sacrificing humanity.

Both modes require boundaries—but different kinds. In founder mode, emotional boundaries are crucial. In manager mode, structural boundaries take center stage. The art is in knowing which role you're in, and adjusting your boundaries accordingly.

Founder Case Studies

- **The Avoidant Leader**: This founder had a tendency to keep people at a distance, focusing heavily on execution while neglecting emotional connection with the team. As a result, employees felt undervalued and trust eroded. Through therapy and intentional vulnerability—such as asking for help and sharing personal challenges in appropriate settings—they began to build authentic relationships and a stronger leadership presence.

- **The Anxious Negotiator**: This founder was paralyzed by investor meetings, constantly second-guessing themselves and seeking reassurance. Through mindfulness practices and the guidance of a seasoned mentor, they developed inner confidence and clarity. With improved self-regulation, they stopped overpromising and began leading conversations from a grounded place of self-worth.

- **The Disorganized Innovator**: A brilliant but chaotic founder swung between micromanaging and disappearing. Their team struggled to know what to expect. With support from an executive coach, they built routines—like weekly check-ins and task prioritization—and learned how to communicate clearly. Stability became their superpower, empowering the entire team to move more effectively.

Curating Your Environment for Boundaries

Patagonia's Purpose-Driven Culture By aligning the company with environmental values, Patagonia attracts a like-minded community. This alignment creates automatic boundaries—people know what to expect and how to show up.

Design Your Workspace

- Remove clutter.
- Add intentional design features (lighting, nature, color).
- Create zones for deep work, collaboration, and rest.

Build Your Support Network

- Identify your go-to mentors, peers, and friends.
- Audit your inner circle: Who drains you? Who energizes you?
- Create boundaries with energy-drainers, even if it's family.

Final Word

Healthy boundaries are a cornerstone of resilience. They help founders stay centered amidst chaos, protect their energy for what matters most, and lead with greater clarity and confidence. When you set and honor boundaries, you create space not just for productivity, but for peace.

Reflection Prompt: Where in your life are you overextending? What boundary, if established, would give you back time, energy, or joy?

Boundaries are not selfish—they are sacred. They are the infrastructure of your inner peace and the container for your greatest work.

Discover Your Founder Attachment Style

Instructions

1. Read each statement below and decide if it applies to you in the context of your founder relationships. If the statement is true for you, place a checkmark (✓) in the column corresponding to that attachment style: Secure, Anxious, Avoidant, or Disorganized.
2. At the end, count the checkmarks in each column. The column with the highest number of checkmarks indicates the attachment style you most align with.
3. Use the results to better understand how your attachment style may influence your decisions, relationships, and resilience as a founder.

Why Understanding Attachment Styles Matters

Attachment styles influence how you handle relationships, stress, and setbacks as a founder. Knowing your style can:

- Enhance communication and trust within teams.
- Help you recognize and address potential biases in decision-making.
- Empower you to build healthier professional and personal relationships.

Question	Secure	Anxious	Avoidant	Disor-ganized
1. I trust my team to make decisions without constant oversight.	✓			
2. I often feel insecure about whether my team truly values me.		✓		
3. I avoid sharing too much of my personal challenges with my team.			✓	
4. I sometimes experience mixed feelings, such as wanting to trust my team but also feeling hesitant to rely on them.				✓
5. I feel confident in delegating responsibilities to others.	✓			
6. I frequently seek reassurance from others about my decisions.		✓		
7. I prefer to handle most challenges on my own rather than asking for help.			✓	
8. I sometimes feel overwhelmed by conflicting emotions when managing team conflicts.				✓

9. I feel comfortable discussing both successes and failures openly with my team.	✓			
10. I worry that others might leave me or abandon the project.		✓		
11. I often distance myself from emotional discussions in the workplace.			✓	
12. I sometimes feel paralyzed when I need to address a team member's poor performance.				✓
13. I believe building trust and transparency is critical for success.	✓			
14. I feel anxious when I don't receive immediate responses from my team.		✓		
15. I value independence and sometimes prefer to work alone even in team settings.			✓	
16. I occasionally struggle with trusting others' intentions in the workplace.				✓

#	Statement				
17.	I handle constructive criticism calmly and use it to improve.	✓			
18.	I feel overly responsible for ensuring everyone on the team feels happy.			✓	
19.	I prefer to keep emotional boundaries in professional relationships.				✓	
20.	I sometimes second-guess whether I made the right hiring decisions.					✓
21.	I feel secure in my ability to manage interpersonal challenges within my team.	✓				
22.	I worry that conflicts in the workplace mean people dislike me.			✓		
23.	I am uncomfortable when others rely too heavily on me emotionally.				✓	
24.	I feel unsure about my ability to lead when things become emotionally tense.					✓
25.	I celebrate my team's successes without feeling overshadowed.	✓				

26. I sometimes feel jealous or uneasy about the close relationships between other team members.		✓		
27. I keep conversations with team members strictly focused on tasks.			✓	
28. I feel unsure how to respond when others seek emotional support from me.				✓
29. I encourage collaboration and value input from all team members.	✓			
30. I worry excessively about whether my team respects my leadership.		✓		
31. I avoid situations where I might need to rely on someone else for help.			✓	
32. I feel conflicted between wanting close relationships and fearing being hurt by them.				✓
33. I feel confident that others will follow through on their commitments.	✓			
34. I get upset when others don't notice my contributions or hard work.		✓		

#	Statement				
35.	I keep a firm line between personal and professional aspects of my life.			✓	
36.	I sometimes feel frozen or unsure how to proceed when things go wrong in relationships.				✓
37.	I feel secure in my ability to handle difficult conversations with my team.	✓			
38.	I feel deeply hurt by even mild criticism or perceived rejection.		✓		
39.	I find it hard to trust others with sensitive or emotional information.			✓	
40.	I find myself alternating between feeling trusting and distrustful of the same person.				✓

What's Next?

Once you've identified your attachment style, reflect on how it influences your leadership. Recognizing these patterns can help you:

- Leverage the strengths of your style to foster stronger relationships.

- Address challenges by adopting strategies that balance emotions and logic.
- Build a more cohesive and supportive team dynamic, ensuring both personal and professional growth.

CHAPTER 13
HARNESSING WEALTH RESILIENCE

In a world marked by inflation, geopolitical instability, and institutional distrust, wealth resilience has become more than a financial strategy—it's a foundation of sovereignty and autonomy. For founders and purpose-driven leaders, financial independence isn't about greed—it's about freedom. The freedom to say no to misaligned investors, to weather turbulent markets, and to stay rooted in your mission, even when the world feels unsteady.

Redefining Wealth Resilience Through the H.E.R.O. Lens

Within the H.E.R.O. framework—Health, Economics, Relationships, and Opportunity—economic resilience is the keystone that empowers the other pillars. Without financial sovereignty, even the most brilliant ideas or purpose-driven ventures are vulnerable to collapse under external pressures. Wealth resilience means building systems that allow you to adapt, grow, and sustain your values regardless of economic or institutional conditions.

The Pillars of Wealth Resilience

1. Diversification and Asset Protection

Wealth resilience begins with intelligent diversification across asset classes, income streams, and geographies.

- **Multiple Income Streams**: Combine employment income, consulting, digital products, investments, real estate, and royalties. The more diverse the cash flow, the less vulnerable you are to any one stream drying up.
- **Strategic Asset Allocation**: Blend traditional assets (stocks, real estate) with alternative assets (Bitcoin, private equity, commodities) to reduce risk exposure.
- **Emergency Fund**: A 3–6 month cash buffer gives you the power to pivot without panic.
- **Risk Management**: Protect your capital through insurance, trusts, legal structures, and estate planning.

2. Inflation Hedging and Long-Term Growth

Your wealth must grow faster than the rate of currency devaluation.

- **Appreciating Assets**: Own assets that historically outperform inflation, such as real estate, equities, and Bitcoin.
- **Entrepreneurship**: Build businesses that scale beyond your time and physical presence.
- **Skill Stacking**: Invest in skills that unlock new income potential—copywriting, coding, leadership, investing.
- **Tax Optimization**: Maximize returns using retirement accounts, LLCs, charitable giving, and legal deductions.

3. Financial Sovereignty and Minimalism

Simplicity is a superpower in uncertain times.

- **Debt Elimination**: Remove high-interest obligations to free up cash flow.
- **Purposeful Spending**: Reduce lifestyle inflation. Buy assets, not liabilities.
- **Passive Income**: Build revenue that doesn't require daily labor—through rental properties, dividend stocks, content licensing, or royalties.

4. Global Mobility and Adaptability

Plan for the unexpected. Future-proof your lifestyle.

- **Geographic Arbitrage**: Live in lower-cost regions while earning in stronger currencies.
- **Internationalization**: Diversify banking, citizenship, and assets across multiple jurisdictions.
- **Digital Freedom**: Build location-independent income streams that allow you to thrive from anywhere.

Bitcoin: The Linchpin of Modern Wealth Resilience

Bitcoin is not just another asset—it's an entirely new paradigm of money. It represents the intersection of technology, scarcity, decentralization, and self-sovereignty. For the resilient founder, Bitcoin is both a hedge and a tool—a financial lifeboat in a sea of systemic risk.

What Makes Bitcoin Unique?

- **Fixed Supply**: Only 21 million Bitcoin will ever exist, protecting against inflationary devaluation.
- **Decentralization**: No government, bank, or institution controls it.
- **Self-Custody**: You can store and access your wealth without permission or intermediaries.
- **Borderless**: Transfer large sums of value anywhere in the world in minutes.
- **Censorship-Resistant**: Bitcoin transactions cannot be reversed, frozen, or denied by third parties.

Hash Rate and Network Security

Bitcoin's hash rate—a measure of the computational power securing the network—continues to rise, even amidst market crashes or government crackdowns. When China banned mining in 2021, the network quickly redistributed and bounced back stronger than ever. This resilience is unmatched in traditional systems.

Actionable Bitcoin Integration for Founders

- **Start with Education**: Learn the basics—what is a wallet, how to store keys, how to send and receive Bitcoin.
- **Dollar-Cost Average (DCA)**: Contribute a small, consistent amount each week or month. Ignore the short-term noise.
- **Cold Storage**: Secure your holdings in a hardware wallet. Avoid keeping Bitcoin on exchanges.
- **Use It**: Experiment with transactions—buy products, send to friends, tip creators.
- **Incorporate in Business**: Accept Bitcoin as payment. Diversify treasury holdings.

Real-World Examples of Bitcoin Resilience

- **El Salvador**: Saved millions in remittance fees and bank access by adopting Bitcoin.
- **Venezuela**: Used as a store of value amidst 1,000,000%+ inflation.
- **Nigeria**: Youth-led adoption of Bitcoin to escape restrictive monetary policy.
- **Ukraine**: Refugees used Bitcoin to access money after losing bank access during the war.

Bitcoin protects against inflation, authoritarianism, and financial censorship—while offering a new level of mobility, autonomy, and trustless transactions.

Designing Your Wealth Resilience Playbook

- **Audit Dependencies**: Where are you overly reliant—on fiat currency, centralized apps, or a single employer or platform?
- **Stack Skills**: Build value creation skills—investing, content creation, tech fluency, leadership.
- **Build Your Digital Wallet**: Learn how to send, receive, and store Bitcoin securely.
- **Embrace Parallel Economies**: Participate in decentralized finance, crypto commerce, and open networks.
- **Plan B**: Secure dual residencies or passports, international bank accounts, or access to crypto-friendly jurisdictions.

Final Word: True Wealth Is the Ability to Choose

Wealth resilience is not merely about accumulating assets. It's about having choices. It's the ability to walk away from coercion, to fund your mission without compromise, and to protect what you've built across generations.

Cryptocurrencies—especially Bitcoin—offer leverage, protection, and unprecedented levels of freedom. In an era of uncertainty, they are no longer fringe. They are essential.

Reflection Prompt: What percentage of your net worth is truly sovereign—owned outright, permissionless, and portable? What's stopping you from increasing it?

CHAPTER 14
FOUNDER FULLFILLMENT DRIVES BUSINESS SUCCESS

As a founder, it's easy to get caught up in the pressures of growth, competition, and the day-to-day grind of running a business. There's often a focus on achieving revenue targets, scaling operations, and optimizing profits. However, one of the most powerful and overlooked factors driving long-term business success is the personal fulfillment of the founder. The internal drive, sense of purpose, and overall happiness of the person behind the company directly affect not only their well-being but also the success of their business.

The Founder's Fulfillment as a Key to Business Growth

Fulfillment as a founder doesn't simply mean "being happy" in a surface-level sense. It goes much deeper—it's about feeling connected to your purpose, being in alignment with your values, and experiencing a sense of meaning in both your personal life and your business endeavors. This deep fulfillment enables you to show up as a leader who is passionate, focused, and driven, which in turn positively impacts the culture, productivity, and innovation within your company.

Founders who operate from a place of fulfillment are more resilient in the face of challenges, more inspiring to their teams, and more capable of sustaining long-term success. Fulfillment fosters a positive feedback loop: when you feel good about what you're doing and aligned with your purpose, it not only motivates you to work harder, but it also inspires others to follow your lead, creating a culture of enthusiasm and commitment.

Key Insights from Founders: Personal Fulfillment Drives Success

The founders we interviewed all shared similar insights about how their personal fulfillment influenced the success of their businesses. Here are a few key takeaways:

1. Purpose Drives Passion

Many of the founders we spoke to cited a clear sense of purpose as one of the driving forces behind their success. When your business is aligned with your personal values and passions, work no longer feels like "work." It becomes a means of self-expression, a platform for achieving something meaningful, and a source of deep personal satisfaction.

For example, Anna, the founder of an eco-friendly skincare company, shared how her love for sustainability and natural health drove her to create products that aligned with her core values. This sense of purpose fueled her passion, helped her persevere through the early struggles, and attracted customers who resonated with her mission.

Actionable Takeaway: To align your business with your personal fulfillment, identify the core values and passions that drive you. Then, ask yourself: How can my business serve not only my financial goals but also my deeper, more meaningful objectives? When you lead with purpose, success will naturally follow.

2. Fulfillment Reduces Stress and Increases Resilience

Another common theme among successful founders was that fulfillment helped them navigate the inevitable stress and obstacles of entrepreneurship. When you're pursuing something that aligns with your purpose, you're far less likely to feel overwhelmed by challenges. Rather than focusing on the hardships, fulfilled founders often see setbacks as valuable lessons or stepping stones toward a greater goal.

David, who founded a technology startup, explained that his sense of fulfillment helped him handle the rollercoaster ride of scaling his business. "When you're truly passionate about what you're building, even the most difficult problems seem like an exciting puzzle to solve," he said.

Actionable Takeaway: To build your resilience, focus on the aspects of your business that ignite your passion. Shift your mindset to view challenges as opportunities for growth. When you're aligned with your purpose, setbacks become less daunting.

3. Fulfilled Founders Create a Thriving Company Culture

Founders who feel fulfilled in their own lives tend to create a thriving company culture. When you're energized by your own sense of purpose and inner satisfaction, that energy ripples out to your employees, investors, and customers. Employees who are led by a passionate, fulfilled founder are more likely to feel inspired, loyal, and committed to the company's mission.

For instance, Carlos, the founder of a socially-conscious coffee company, emphasized how his personal fulfillment with his business mission translated into a company culture built on shared values. "Our team is driven by something bigger than just profits. They care about the impact we're making in the world, and that sense of purpose unites us," he said.

Actionable Takeaway: Be transparent about your personal mission and how it aligns with your company's values. Share your passion with your team and encourage them to find meaning in their work. When you build a purpose-driven company culture, it becomes a powerful driver of engagement, innovation, and retention.

The Business Benefits of Personal Fulfillment

Beyond the personal satisfaction that fulfillment brings, there are clear business benefits as well. The following points illustrate how fulfillment impacts the success of your business:

1. Improved Decision-Making

When you're fulfilled, you have clarity about your long-term goals and priorities. This clarity helps you make better, more aligned decisions—whether it's about product development, partnerships, or company strategy. Founders who are connected to their values are less likely to be swayed by short-term trends or external pressures that could lead them off course.

Actionable Takeaway: When faced with a tough decision, ask yourself: Does this align with my core values and the larger purpose of my business? By making decisions from a place of fulfillment, you ensure that every move you make is aligned with your true vision.

2. Enhanced Creativity and Innovation

Personal fulfillment enhances your creativity and problem-solving abilities. When you feel good about the work you're doing, you are more open to new ideas and more willing to take calculated risks. Fulfilled founders are often more innovative because they operate from a space of abundance, optimism, and possibility.

Actionable Takeaway: Nurture your creativity by consistently working on projects that energize and inspire you. Take time to explore new ideas, experiment, and challenge yourself to think outside the box. This will lead to innovative solutions and breakthroughs for your business.

3. Stronger Relationships with Customers and Stakeholders

When you're fulfilled, your authenticity shines through in every interaction. Customers are drawn to businesses that have an authentic mission and a founder who genuinely cares about their needs. Fulfillment creates an atmosphere of trust, which strengthens relationships with customers, investors, and business partners.

Actionable Takeaway: Be authentic in your business interactions. Share your story, values, and the mission behind your business with your customers. The more transparent and genuine you are, the stronger the connection you'll build with your audience.

How to Cultivate Fulfillment as a Founder

While fulfillment is a deeply personal experience, there are concrete actions you can take to cultivate it in your own life. Here are a few strategies that successful founders use to stay aligned with their purpose and maintain fulfillment:

1. Align Your Work with Your Values

Regularly check in with your personal values and ensure that your business is aligned with them. Ask yourself, "What are the core principles that guide my decisions?" Ensure your company's mission, products, and culture reflect these values.

2. Prioritize Personal Well-Being

Taking care of yourself is essential for fulfillment. Make time for physical health, emotional well-being, and mental clarity. Regular exercise, meditation, journaling, and time for hobbies outside of work can help you stay grounded and fulfilled.

3. Cultivate Meaningful Relationships

Fulfillment often comes from meaningful human connections. Build a strong network of mentors, peers, and friends who can support you emotionally and professionally. Nurture relationships with your team and customers to create a sense of community around your business.

4. Celebrate Your Achievements

Acknowledging your accomplishments, both big and small, reinforces the feeling of fulfillment. Take time to celebrate milestones, reflect on your progress, and appreciate how far you've come in your journey.

The link between a founder's fulfillment and business success is undeniable. When you are aligned with your purpose, values, and passions, you bring a sense of energy, clarity, and resilience to your business. Fulfillment not only drives personal well-being but also fosters a thriving company culture, enhances decision-making, and inspires creativity.

As a founder, your happiness and satisfaction are not separate from the success of your business—they are deeply interconnected. By nurturing your fulfillment, you empower your business to grow and flourish, creating lasting success for yourself, your team, and your customers.

In the next chapter, we will explore The Modern-Day Founder's Blueprint, outlining practical steps for leading like a founder, not a manager. This blueprint will help you scale your business while staying true to your purpose and maintaining your fulfillment.

CHAPTER 15
THE MODERN-DAY FOUNDER'S BLUEPRINT

How to Lead Like a Founder, Not a Manager

In today's rapidly changing business environment, the role of the founder has evolved. Traditional management advice often centers around structured hierarchies, command-and-control systems, and top-down decision-making. While these approaches can work in certain contexts, they tend to be limiting for founders who are aiming to build businesses that are both impactful and sustainable.

The modern-day founder is not just a manager but a leader who is deeply connected to the vision and purpose of the company. A founder's leadership style should be rooted in the same values and passion that inspired the creation of the business. It is a leadership style that is flexible, purpose-driven, and focused on long-term goals.

In this chapter, we will explore the core components of the modern-day founder's leadership blueprint. We'll cover how to lead with authenticity, empower your team, and make decisions that align with your deeper purpose—all while fostering growth and innovation in your company.

The Essence of Leading Like a Founder

At the heart of founder-led businesses is a vision that transcends day-to-day operations. Founders who lead from this place of purpose and vision are able to inspire their teams, guide strategic decisions, and create cultures that resonate with both employees and customers. Unlike managers, whose roles often focus on maintaining efficiency and managing processes, founders are builders of the future—they drive the vision, make bold decisions, and take calculated risks that push the company forward.

Key Characteristics of a Founder's Leadership Style:

1. Visionary Leadership

A modern-day founder leads with a clear and compelling vision. This vision is not just a business goal, but a broader mission that aligns with the founder's personal values. Visionary leadership empowers the team by providing clarity about where the company is headed and why it matters.

For example, consider Elon Musk at Tesla. His vision of creating a sustainable future through electric cars has guided not only Tesla's innovations but also the broader shift in the automotive industry. His leadership is rooted in a larger purpose, and that purpose motivates his team to work toward a collective goal.

Actionable Takeaway: As a founder, craft a compelling vision for your company. This vision should align with your values and inspire your team. Keep your focus on the long-term, and remember that your vision will evolve as your company grows.

2. Authenticity

Founders who lead authentically are more trusted, respected, and admired by their teams. Authenticity comes from being true to who you are, embracing your strengths and weaknesses, and openly sharing your personal journey. When your team sees you as an authentic leader, they are more likely to follow your example, feel motivated, and take ownership of their work.

A great example of this is Richard Branson, the founder of Virgin Group, who has built his brand around being authentic, approachable, and transparent. Branson's openness about his struggles, successes, and values has helped him form deep connections with his employees and customers alike.

Actionable Takeaway: Lead by example. Share your authentic self with your team. Be transparent about both the challenges and the successes you face. Your authenticity will foster trust and loyalty, encouraging your team to fully engage in your mission.

3. Empowerment and Trust

The modern-day founder understands that they cannot do everything themselves. Instead of micromanaging, founders empower their team members by delegating responsibility and trusting them to make decisions. This not only builds a strong sense of ownership within the company but also allows the founder to focus on strategic decisions and innovation.

Take a look at Steve Jobs, who famously trusted his team of engineers and designers at Apple to develop cutting-edge products. Jobs empowered his team to think outside the box and challenge the status quo—allowing Apple to create revolutionary products like the iPhone.

Actionable Takeaway: Trust your team to deliver on your vision. Hire people who align with your values and give them the autonomy to make decisions. This will not only increase the capacity of your business but also inspire innovation from within.

4. Resilience and Adaptability

A modern-day founder is resilient in the face of challenges and adaptable when the business environment changes. Founders often face uncertainty, competition, and setbacks. The ability to stay flexible, pivot when necessary, and adapt to new circumstances is a key component of successful founder leadership.

For example, Jeff Bezos's decision to transition Amazon from an online bookstore to a global e-commerce giant shows the adaptability of founder-led companies. Bezos constantly iterated on Amazon's business model, innovating in response to changing market demands and consumer behavior.

Actionable Takeaway: Develop a mindset of resilience and adaptability. Be willing to pivot and innovate as your business evolves. Recognize that setbacks are opportunities for learning and growth, not signals to give up.

Key Leadership Strategies for the Modern-Day Founder

Now that we've explored the core characteristics of a founder's leadership style, let's dive into actionable strategies that can help you lead like a modern-day founder.

1. Focus on Purpose-Driven Leadership

Purpose-driven leadership isn't just about profit—it's about making an impact. As a founder, your leadership should be deeply connected to the broader mission of your company. This mission should be at the core of every decision, from product development to marketing strategies.

Actionable Takeaway: Regularly revisit your company's mission statement and ensure it aligns with your personal values. Communicate your mission clearly and consistently to your team, customers, and stakeholders. Make sure every decision you make ties back to your larger purpose.

2. Implement Skip-Level Meetings

Skip-level meetings are a great way to foster transparency, trust, and open communication within your organization. These meetings occur between you (the founder) and employees who are several levels below you in the organizational hierarchy. This gives you the opportunity to hear directly from team members, understand their challenges, and foster a culture of collaboration and innovation.

A well-known example of this is Google, where founders Larry Page and Sergey Brin often held skip-level meetings with employees. This helped them stay connected to the company's culture and foster a sense of community within the organization.

Actionable Takeaway: Schedule regular skip-level meetings with employees at all levels. Use these meetings as opportunities to listen, gather feedback, and inspire your team with your vision.

3. Maintain Deep Involvement in the Operations

While delegation is important, it's also crucial to stay involved in the day-to-day operations of your business. As a founder, you need to keep a pulse on the company's activities to ensure that they align with your vision. This deep involvement doesn't mean micromanaging—it means staying engaged with your team, understanding the challenges they face, and offering guidance when necessary.

Actionable Takeaway: Set aside time to regularly engage with key operational areas of your business. Participate in product development meetings, sales reviews, or customer feedback sessions to stay connected with your company's core functions.

4. Lead with Empathy and Emotional Intelligence

Empathy and emotional intelligence (EQ) are critical traits for a founder's leadership. Leading with empathy allows you to connect with your team on a deeper level and foster a positive work environment. A leader with high EQ is better able to navigate interpersonal dynamics, resolve conflicts, and motivate their team.

Actionable Takeaway: Work on improving your emotional intelligence by practicing active listening, understanding the needs of your team members, and responding to challenges with empathy and understanding. When your team feels heard and valued, they will be more motivated and loyal.

5. Commit to Continuous Learning and Growth

The best leaders are always learning. Whether it's through reading, attending workshops, or seeking mentorship, a modern-day founder should commit to ongoing personal and professional development. This learning mindset not only helps you grow as a leader but also sets an example for your team.

Actionable Takeaway: Commit to continuous learning by setting aside time each week to expand your knowledge. Seek feedback from your team, read books and articles, or enroll in leadership courses. Your growth as a leader will directly benefit your business.

Reinventing Work Culture: Lessons from Netflix and Reed Hastings

One of the most transformative examples of modern leadership comes from Netflix under the guidance of its co-founder and former CEO, Reed Hastings. In the book *No Rules Rules*, Hastings outlines the unconventional yet highly effective strategies Netflix employed to create a high-performing work culture. By prioritizing freedom and responsibility over traditional hierarchical control, Netflix was able to innovate, grow, and consistently stay ahead of competitors.

Netflix's journey offers invaluable lessons for founders aiming to build dynamic, adaptable, and highly productive organizations.

Key Principles of Netflix's Work Culture

1. **Freedom with Responsibility**

    Netflix's culture is built on the idea that employees perform best when given the freedom to make decisions.

Hastings and his team abandoned traditional corporate policies, such as strict vacation policies or expense controls, trusting employees to act in the company's best interests. This freedom not only empowered employees but also encouraged them to think and act like owners of the business.

Actionable Takeaway: Simplify or eliminate restrictive policies where possible. Trust your team to make the right decisions and hold them accountable for results rather than processes.

2. **Radical Candor and Transparency**

   Open and honest communication is a cornerstone of Netflix's culture. Employees are encouraged to provide direct feedback to their peers and managers, fostering a culture of continuous improvement. Hastings emphasizes the importance of radical candor to ensure that problems are addressed swiftly and openly.

   Actionable Takeaway: Create an environment where feedback is normalized and encouraged. Lead by example by being open to receiving and giving constructive feedback.

3. **Building a Talent-Dense Team**

   Hastings championed the concept of a "talent density" culture, where the focus is on hiring and retaining the most talented individuals. Netflix's philosophy is to compensate top performers generously and let go of those who are not meeting high standards, even if they are performing adequately. This ensures that every team member is highly skilled and fully committed to driving the company's vision forward.

   Actionable Takeaway: Prioritize hiring top talent and focus on continuous performance evaluations. Be prepared to make tough decisions to maintain a high-performing team.

4. **Encouraging Innovation Through Context, Not Control**

   Rather than micromanaging, Netflix leaders focus on setting clear goals and providing context for their decisions. This approach allows team members to innovate and problem-solve independently, fostering creativity and ownership.

   Actionable Takeaway: Clearly communicate the "why" behind decisions and objectives. Encourage your team to find solutions rather than prescribing how tasks should be accomplished.

5. **Embracing Adaptability**

   Hastings understood that the entertainment industry is constantly evolving, and he built Netflix's culture to thrive in change. The company frequently reevaluates its strategies and pivots when necessary, staying ahead of technological and consumer trends.

   Actionable Takeaway: Build adaptability into your leadership style. Be prepared to pivot and innovate as your industry evolves, and encourage your team to embrace change as an opportunity rather than a challenge.

How Netflix Reinvented Productivity

Netflix's cultural transformation allowed the company to achieve remarkable productivity and innovation. By focusing on freedom, transparency, and talent density, Netflix created an environment where employees were not only more effective but also more motivated and engaged.

Integration into the Founder's Blueprint:

Reed Hastings' approach underscores the importance of aligning company culture with your broader vision. For founders, this means creating an organizational culture that mirrors the values and principles driving your mission. By prioritizing trust, autonomy, and adaptability, you can build a resilient and forward-thinking team that's ready to tackle the challenges of the modern business world.

Actionable Takeaways:

- Reassess your company's policies and practices to identify areas where you can foster more freedom and responsibility.
- Cultivate a culture of radical candor, where employees feel empowered to speak openly and honestly.
- Focus on building a high-performance team by investing in top talent and continuously refining your team's capabilities.
- Encourage innovation by providing context for decisions and trusting your team to execute effectively.

By adopting these principles, you can create a workplace culture that is not only productive but also deeply aligned with your company's vision and purpose.

CHAPTER 16
SCALING WITH PURPOSE

Sustaining Founder H.E.R.O. as Your Company Grows

Scaling a business is more than just increasing revenue or hiring new team members—it's about growing without losing your soul. As a founder, you've poured time, vision, sweat, and spirit into building something that matters. But when your startup becomes a scaling company, the original spark that gave birth to your mission is often tested. The key challenge is this: How do you maintain alignment with your original purpose while empowering others to lead and execute at scale?

This chapter explores how to scale your company with intention using the Founder H.E.R.O. framework—Health, Economics, Relationships, and Opportunity—so you don't lose yourself or your vision in the process. Scaling with purpose is about staying anchored in your values, reinforcing your mission, and fostering a culture that grows stronger, not diluted, as your business evolves.

The Scaling Dilemma: Losing Purpose in Growth

Growth introduces complexity: new teams, stakeholders, technologies, and expectations. This can push founders into "manager mode," where the focus becomes systems and processes rather than people and purpose. While operations matter, founders must also remain in their visionary role—what we call "Founder Mode."

The H.E.R.O. framework serves as a compass. By ensuring health, economics, relationships, and opportunity remain aligned with your mission, you create a business that scales sustainably—without sacrificing what made it special to begin with.

1. Health: Sustainable Leadership Starts with You

The stress of growth can erode your well-being, which in turn impacts your ability to lead. Founders who neglect physical, mental, or emotional health risk burnout—and burnout founders can't build resilient businesses.

H.E.R.O. Health in Action:

- Establish non-negotiable health routines: exercise, sleep, nutrition, and mindfulness.
- Schedule white space in your calendar for reflection and recovery.
- Model work-life balance and build a company culture that promotes wellness.

Founder Insight: A founder who scaled a 10-person team to 100 said, "The more people I managed, the more essential it became for me to protect my mornings for physical movement and meditation. That hour gave me clarity and emotional stamina."

2. Economics: Scaling with Financial Integrity

Rapid growth can tempt you to chase revenue at the expense of sustainability. Purpose-driven founders must think long-term, designing business models that honor the mission and ensure financial health.

H.E.R.O. Economics in Action:

- Invest in systems and talent that enable profitable, scalable operations.
- Resist the pressure to overextend. Not every shiny opportunity is worth the risk.
- Align your pricing, margins, and monetization strategy with your values.

Pro Tip: Apply constraint-based thinking. Instead of asking, "How do we grow at all costs?" ask, "How do we grow profitably and stay mission-aligned?"

3. Relationships: Culture and Connection at Scale

As companies grow, founders naturally spend less time with each individual employee. But this doesn't mean your influence should diminish. Scaling your presence means designing culture intentionally.

H.E.R.O. Relationships in Action:

- Build leadership pipelines by mentoring others to carry the mission.

- Hold regular all-hands and team meetings focused on vision and values.
- Maintain transparency, even when it's uncomfortable. People respect honest leadership.

Founder Case Study: The co-founders of a growing B2B SaaS company held quarterly "Founder Firesides" where they shared origin stories, answered questions, and reinforced the company's values—even as the team surpassed 200 employees.

4. Opportunity: Choose Purpose Over Distraction

As you scale, opportunities flood in—new markets, partnerships, acquisitions. But not every opportunity is aligned with your deeper mission. Scaling with purpose means filtering opportunities through your "why."

H.E.R.O. Opportunity in Action:

- Create an opportunity filter—does this align with our core values, vision, and customer promise?
- Empower your team to recognize and act on aligned opportunities.
- Say no—often. Clarity of mission sharpens your ability to discern what matters.

Strategy Tip: Use the Eisenhower Matrix (urgent vs. important) to filter noise and double down on what truly moves your mission forward.

Scaling with Integrity: Lessons from Purpose-Driven Brands

Airbnb

- As Airbnb scaled globally, it anchored its brand on one powerful idea: "Belong anywhere."
- They reinforced this purpose through customer experiences, trust-building features, and localized community support.

Warby Parker

- Their "Buy a Pair, Give a Pair" program stayed at the heart of their business—even as they expanded into retail and IPO.
- They trained employees on the company's social mission and made customer impact a core KPI.

Lesson: When values are woven into your culture, product, and growth strategy, scale becomes an amplifier—not a dilution—of purpose.

Aligning with Simon Sinek's Start with Why

Simon Sinek's concept—that people don't buy what you do, they buy why you do it—remains a powerful reminder as you grow. Integrating the "why" into the H.E.R.O. framework ensures you scale with clarity, not just complexity.

- **Health**: Reconnect with your personal "why." Protect your energy so your passion remains strong.
- **Economics**: Design your growth strategy to reflect your deeper purpose, not just profit.

- **Relationships**: Inspire through your values. Lead with purpose to unify your team.
- **Opportunity**: Measure success not only in revenue, but in how closely each new venture aligns with your vision.

Action Prompt: Schedule a quarterly "Why Audit." Revisit your mission. Ask: Are we still aligned? What needs to realign?

Final Thought: Founder H.E.R.O. Isn't Just a Framework—It's a Compass

Scaling with purpose is the real founder's journey. It's the difference between building a company that just works and building a company that matters. The H.E.R.O. framework helps you stay grounded while growing. It reminds you that:

- Health fuels leadership.
- Economics sustains your mission.
- Relationships build culture.
- Opportunities shape your legacy.

Scaling doesn't require you to let go of your identity. It invites you to scale it.

Reflection Prompt:

- What would scaling with integrity look like in my business?
- Where have I sacrificed purpose for growth—and how can I realign?
- How can I lead as a Founder H.E.R.O. through the next stage of growth?

CHAPTER 17
SUSTAINING FOUNDER H.E.R.O

Long-Term Strategies for Personal and Business Resilience

Reaching a revenue milestone or launching a new product may feel like crossing the finish line—but in reality, it's only the beginning. The true challenge lies not in the start-up hustle, but in sustaining the energy, clarity, and purpose that brought you this far. That's where the Founder H.E.R.O. framework—Health, Economics, Relationships, and Opportunities—evolves from a playbook into a way of life.

To thrive long term, founders must continuously cultivate all four resilience domains. Each one is a pillar in the architecture of sustained success—for yourself, your team, and your mission.

1. Build a Practice of Lifelong Learning

Like physical fitness, intellectual and strategic growth require consistent exercise. Continuous learning isn't optional for founders; it's oxygen. Whether you're listening to a podcast on a walk, attending a mastermind, or exploring cutting-edge business models, your capacity to grow defines your ability to lead.

Actionable Insight: Commit to learning one new thing daily—related to health, financial strategy, leadership, or emerging opportunities. Subscribe to industry newsletters, build a curated reading habit, and foster conversations with mentors or peers who stretch your thinking.

2. Establish Sustainable Routines and Keystone Habits

Success doesn't come from heroic effort—it comes from consistent, aligned action. Founders who last build simple, repeatable routines that protect their energy and mental clarity. These rituals form the backbone of resilience.

Actionable Insight: Design a personal operating system. Incorporate daily movement, sleep hygiene, and nutritional rhythm. Pair these with wealth-building habits like intentional spending reviews, regular portfolio checks, and recurring savings automation. Let your systems do the heavy lifting.

3. Invest in Meaningful Relationships

Relationships are not just your support system—they are your strategic ecosystem. As your business grows, your personal and professional relationships must evolve with it. The people you surround yourself with either drain your energy or multiply it.

Actionable Insight: Create intentional connection points: schedule weekly mentor check-ins, quarterly team retreats, or regular peer mastermind sessions. Seek relationships that challenge you, nurture you, and open doors to new possibilities. Your network is your emotional and strategic safety net.

4. Embrace Flexibility as a Strength, Not a Compromise

Founders who thrive long-term aren't the ones who rigidly stick to a plan—they're the ones who adapt quickly without losing direction. Flexibility is an act of leadership. It's your ability to shift tactics while staying rooted in your values.

Actionable Insight: Build adaptability into your company culture. Encourage experimentation. Develop personal reflection rituals—monthly reviews or feedback sessions—that help you recalibrate strategies across all four domains. Resilience isn't resisting change—it's mastering it.

5. Revisit and Reaffirm Your Purpose

Purpose isn't static—it matures with you. As your business scales and the stakes rise, so must your relationship with your "why." Reconnecting with purpose fuels clarity, refines priorities, and ensures alignment between your mission and your actions.

Actionable Insight: Create a quarterly "founder reflection" ritual. Ask yourself: Does my current path still reflect my core purpose? What needs to realign? Invite your team into this process. When purpose becomes a shared narrative, it becomes an enduring advantage.

6. Design Your Legacy Now

Sustaining Founder H.E.R.O isn't just about staying in the game—it's about leaving a mark. Your legacy is built in the small moments: how you treat your team, the integrity of your decisions, the values embedded in your culture.

Actionable Insight: Craft a personal and organizational legacy plan. Include mentorship, sustainable practices, and generational wealth strategies. Legacy isn't just about what you leave behind—it's about what you build into the future, brick by brick.

Final Thoughts

Sustaining Founder H.E.R.O requires discipline, reflection, and a willingness to evolve. It's a long-game strategy—one that prioritizes aligned growth over burnout, purpose over pressure, and people over performance alone.

You didn't become a founder to create a fragile empire. You stepped into this path to build something that lasts—and that starts with you.

Reflection Prompt: Which domain of Founder H.E.R.O needs your attention most right now? What habit, connection, or perspective shift will strengthen that domain this week?

"Chapter 17: Embrace Founder H.E.R.O Your Journey Begins Now"

Congratulations—you've made it to the final chapter. But this is not the end. It's the beginning of something far more powerful: the daily commitment to live and lead as a Founder H.E.R.O. You've explored the framework of Health, Economics, Relationships, and Opportunities. Now it's time to apply it—not as a checklist, but as a philosophy for life and business.

This chapter is your personal launchpad. It's where preparation meets action, and where vision becomes reality. The Founder H.E.R.O path isn't about perfection. It's about showing up with purpose, every single day.

1. Take Aligned Action

Clarity of purpose is the compass that guides you through the noise and pressure of entrepreneurship. It centers you when decisions get complex and reminds you why you started. Purposeful action turns vision into traction.

Actionable Insight:

Write out your personal mission and your company's "why." Then ask yourself: Do my current behaviors align with these values? Audit your weekly schedule. Identify any actions that drain your energy or pull you out of alignment. Replace them with tasks that fuel your growth across health, wealth, relationships, and opportunity.

2. Build Keystone Habits

Success doesn't come from dramatic changes—it comes from consistent, small steps taken daily. Keystone habits are the foundational routines that, when mastered, positively impact all areas of life.

Actionable Insight:

Pick one habit that touches multiple domains. For example, a 10-minute morning routine that includes breathwork (health), a financial check-in (economics), gratitude texts to a mentor (relationships), and 5 minutes of market reading (opportunities). Start simple. Compound relentlessly.

3. Lead Through Embodiment

Your team is watching. Your clients are listening. Your family is learning. As a founder, you don't just build products—you model possibility. The most powerful leaders don't just talk about values—they live them.

Actionable Insight:

Choose one H.E.R.O. domain to intentionally lead through this week. Prioritize self-care? Share financial transparency? Nurture a strained relationship? Explore a bold opportunity? Make it visible. Invite your team into the process so they're empowered to grow with you.

4. Create Space for Reflection

Resilience is built in the quiet moments. It's in the pause before reaction, the clarity that follows challenge, the insight that comes from slowing down. Regular reflection helps you recognize growth, recalibrate, and recommit.

Actionable Insight:

Create a "Founder H.E.R.O. Journal" and review it weekly. Use four simple prompts:

- What did I do for my health this week?
- How did I grow or protect my wealth?
- Which relationships did I nurture?
- What new opportunities did I explore or act on?

Track progress. Celebrate wins. Refine where needed.

5. Build a Circle That Supports Your Growth

A founder's strength is magnified by their community. The journey is too long, too complex, and too meaningful to travel alone. Curate your inner circle with intention—seek people who challenge you, uplift you, and walk beside you.

Actionable Insight:

Map out your support network. Who is your health accountability partner? Your financial sounding board? Your go-to for honest feedback? If there are gaps, seek new connections—through mastermind groups, local meetups, coaching relationships, or aligned partnerships.

6. Make a Bold Move

While habits build momentum, sometimes a leap is what's needed to create breakthrough. There's likely one decision you've been delaying—because it's hard, scary, or uncertain. But your next evolution might be on the other side of that choice.

Actionable Insight:

Ask yourself: What's the one bold action I've been avoiding that could realign me with my deeper purpose? Then take a step. It might be launching a new offer, letting go of a toxic relationship, hiring support, or prioritizing a health transformation. Boldness brings clarity.

Final Words: You Are the Framework

Founder H.E.R.O. is not a static set of practices. It's a living, breathing framework embodied by you. You don't need to do it perfectly—you just need to commit fully. Let your health be your energy source. Let your economics reflect your freedom. Let your relationships be your roots. Let your opportunities be your wings.

Your journey is not just to build something great—it's to become someone great in the process.

So step forward. You already have everything you need.

Founder H.E.R.O. isn't just a title. It's who you are becoming. Start today.

Reflection Prompt:

What will you do in the next 24 hours to live as a Founder H.E.R.O? Write it down. Make it real. Then act on it. The world is waiting for what only you can build.'"

Ready to Transform Your Purpose into Action?

Join our **Free 7-Day Recon Business LaunchPad Challenge**, designed specifically to help you launch and scale a profitable, service-based business, enhance your online presence, or elevate your non-profit organization using proven, easy-to-follow technology and strategies.

During this impactful 7-day challenge, you'll learn how to:

- Choose a profitable niche and set clear, SMART goals.
- Develop a compelling brand and digital presence.
- Master marketing, lead generation, and SEO strategies.
- Automate your marketing and sales processes with advanced tools like Go High Level.
- Improve your sales skills to confidently close deals.
- Efficiently fulfill services and deliver exceptional customer experiences.
- Set up foundational business operations to scale effectively.

Take your first step toward business success and greater personal fulfillment today: Join the **Free 7-Day Recon Business LaunchPad Challenge** now!

Own Your Purpose

Congratulations, for making it this far in your journey. By now, you've absorbed stories, strategies, and lessons designed to equip you with the resilience, vision, and tools to own your life's purpose. But this journey isn't just about you—it's about the ripple effects you create in your community and beyond.

As you close this book, we have one final ask: Share this book with someone who needs it. Think of that one person in your life who's on the verge of greatness but might need a push. Someone with untapped potential or an unspoken dream. Maybe it's a friend, a family member, or even a colleague. Together, we can build a community of resilient, purpose-driven individuals who inspire and support one another.

At Extreme Resilience, we're not just content with the pages of this book. We're actively working to create tools and resources that empower people like you to thrive. Right now, we're diving deeper into helping individuals find their purpose and build their resilience with our flagship self-guided holistic program. If you enjoyed this book and want to take your journey to the next level, head to extremeresilience.net and use the code FOUNDERHERO (in all caps, one word) to get 50% off our program.

But our mission doesn't stop there. Extreme Resilience is also deeply committed to supporting disaster recovery efforts in Western North Carolina through the nonprofit organization Resilient Recovery NC. Founded in response to Hurricane Helene, this organization provides critical disaster recovery support to rebuild the lives and communities devastated by natural disasters.

Resilient Recovery NC: Restoring Hope and Rebuilding Strength

Resilient Recovery NC is more than just a nonprofit; it's a lifeline for those affected by disasters. Jim & his wife started Resilient Recovery NC as a direct response to the desperate need of relief needed from the flooding that was inflicted on the thousands of victims in Western N.C. Led by Jim, who runs day-to-day operations, and supported by the leadership of our VP (myself), this organization focuses on:

- Aid Distribution: Operating a 500,000 sq. ft. warehouse equipped to organize and distribute relief supplies to affected areas efficiently.
- Debris Cleanup: Utilizing heavy machinery and dedicated volunteers to clear storm damage and restore safe access to communities.
- New Home Construction: Building disaster-resistant, affordable Quonset Hut homes with a 90-day turnaround to provide displaced families with secure shelter.
- Private Road and Bridge Repairs: Restoring vital access points for families affected by storm damage.
- Environmental Restoration: Employing innovative techniques like mycoremediation and phytoremediation to heal damaged ecosystems and rebuild nutrient-rich soils.

The mission of Resilient Recovery NC is to not only help communities recover from disasters but to empower them to thrive in their aftermath. As one community member shared: *"Resilient Recovery NC helped kickstart us back to recovery, not only physically but emotionally and spiritually."*

Resilient Recovery N.C repairing the culvert in the town of Little Switzerland, N.C that was damaged during Hurricane Helene.

How You Can Help

1. Support Resilient Recovery NC: Visit resiliencerecoverync.org to learn more, donate, or volun-

teer. Every contribution helps us rebuild lives and restore hope.

2. Spread the Word: Share this book and the story of Resilient Recovery NC with your network. Awareness is a powerful tool for change.

3. Shop with Purpose: Extreme Resilience is pledging 10% of all profits to support Resilient Recovery NC's efforts. By purchasing our self-guided program or future products like our hydration tea droplets (launching in Q4 of 2025), you're directly contributing to disaster relief and recovery efforts.

Founder H.E.R.O isn't just a book; it's a movement. Together, we can ignite a ripple effect of purpose and resilience that reaches far beyond ourselves. Join us in making an impact—one person, one community, one act of resilience at a time.

Thank you for being part of this journey. Let's build a stronger, more purposeful, and resilient world together.

If you are a founder with a successful business that operates your life & ventures under a similar set of beliefs, head to extremeresilience.net/foundermode we would love to share your journey & story in our next book!

With gratitude,
Jim, Chris, and The Extreme Resilience Team

ACKNOWLEDGMENTS

No entrepreneurial journey is a solo endeavor. While the path of a founder often feels like an isolated pursuit, it is shaped by the wisdom, generosity, and hard-earned insights of those who have walked before us. This book, *Founder H.E.R.O.*, is a culmination of years of learning, failing, adapting, and growing—an evolution made possible by the remarkable thinkers, builders, and mentors who have left an indelible mark on our journey.

We want to extend our deepest gratitude to four individuals whose ideas, philosophies, and actions have profoundly influenced the way we think about entrepreneurship, resilience, and purpose-driven success.

Alex Hormozi – The Relentless Pursuit of Value

Few people embody the principles of **long-term thinking, value creation, and entrepreneurial resilience** like Alex Hormozi. His unwavering commitment to playing the infinite game of business—focusing on skills, reputation, and impact over short-term gains—has been a guiding philosophy for us. Through his books, content, and personal journey, Alex has demonstrated that resilience is not about enduring hardship for its own sake but about becoming the kind of person who can thrive in any environment. His insights on **stacking leverage, mastering the fundamentals, and showing up consistently** have shaped how we approach both our ventures and this book.

Alberto Savoia – Testing, Iterating, and The Right It

The impact of **Alberto Savoia's** work, particularly *The Right It*, cannot be overstated. His philosophy on **pretoyping**—validating ideas before overcommitting resources—has transformed the way we approach risk and decision-making. The notion that **failure is not an option, but failing to test is** has instilled in us a deeper respect for data-driven experimentation. In a world where founders often romanticize their ideas, Alberto has reminded us that **resilience is not about stubbornly holding on to a flawed vision, but about having the courage to adapt and iterate**. His work has given us the tools to move forward with conviction while maintaining the humility to pivot when necessary.

Adam Fletcher – Resilience Is Not a Currency

The idea that **resilience is not a currency** but rather a muscle to be trained is something we first encountered through **Adam Fletcher and The Fletcher Method**. In a world where hustle culture often glorifies burnout, Adam's perspective has helped us redefine what it truly means to be a resilient founder. His structured approach to business building, marketing, and systems-thinking has reinforced that **entrepreneurial success is not about grinding endlessly but about creating repeatable, scalable frameworks that allow you to sustain momentum.** His influence has been instrumental in shaping the H.E.R.O. framework, particularly in how we think about **Economic and Opportunity resilience.**

Wes Bergmann – The Blox & the Power of Entrepreneurial Community

Finally, a massive thank you to **Wes Bergmann** for creating *The Blox*—an environment where ambitious founders could test themselves against real challenges while forging relationships with like-minded visionaries. Being part of Season 3 was a transformational experience, exposing us to **new perspectives, competitive collaboration, and the power of shared entrepreneurial passion**. More than a competition, *The Blox* was a proving ground for ideas, resilience, and execution. Wes, your ability to create a space where founders can push their limits while supporting one another has left a lasting impact on how we view **entrepreneurial ecosystems and the importance of community.**

Gratitude & Paying It Forward

To these four incredible thinkers, doers, and trailblazers—thank you. Your work has shaped not only our journey but the insights within this book. We hope that *Founder H.E.R.O.* serves as a continuation of the conversations you started, helping more entrepreneurs build resilience, create impact, and, most importantly, **own their purpose.**

Special Thanks to Rena Coll

I want to express my deepest gratitude to the most resilient mother I could ever ask for. Your unwavering support has been the foundation of my journey, shaping me into the person I am today. Raising two relentless boys—who, as my Dad would say, "I saw less fighting in Afghanistan"—was no small feat, yet you handled it with strength, patience, and an unshakable sense of love.

Your dedication to your work and your relentless perseverance have been my greatest source of inspiration.

Watching you lead by example instilled in me the discipline, resilience, and work ethic that drive me every day. I am who I am because of you.

No matter where life takes us, I will always be there for you—just as you have always been there for me.

Tribute to Philip Fischer (Chris' Uncle)

There are people in our lives who shape us in ways we can never fully put into words—mentors, role models, and unwavering supporters who leave an imprint on our hearts. My Uncle Phil was all of these and more. He was not just my uncle; he was my second dad, my coach, my best friend, and a guiding force in my life.

For over 35 years, he dedicated himself to teaching middle school history. Uncle Phil's generosity knew no limits. Whether on the field as a coach or in everyday life as a friend, he was always there—lifting others up, offering wisdom, and leading by example. His sudden passing in December of 2024 left a void that can never truly be filled, but his impact will live on through the countless lives he touched.

I will never forget you, Uncle Phil. Your kindness, your wisdom, and your unwavering belief in me will stay with me forever.

Special Thanks to Rebekah Artman

To my wife, Rebekah Artman—thank you for embodying what it means to be resilient, as my wife, mother, daughter and aspiring hospital CEO. Watching you lead everyday from your heart, with the courage to be authentic, candid, and committed to being there for your staff is inspiring to watch. The probably hundreds of late night conversations we've had about shifting culture and corporate leadership has directly impacted the direction of some of the research that went into this book. Your journey from CNA to Chief Nursing Officer is a testament to your resilience, determination, and deep compassion for both patients and colleagues. You inspire me every day with your ability to lift others, empower teams, and transform challenges into opportunities for growth.

This book wouldn't exist without your unwavering support and belief in my vision. You remind me constantly of the strength found in humility and the power of servant leadership. Thank you for being my greatest champion and the cornerstone of our family's own journey in resilience and purpose.

Shane Hazel & Bitcoin Veterans

Shane Hazel & Bitcoin: A heartfelt thank you to Shane Hazel and Bitcoin Veterans for their unwavering commitment to wealth resilience and the promotion of freedom through cryptocurrency. Shane, your passion for empowering individuals to take control of their financial futures through Bitcoin is inspiring, and your dedication to advancing decentralized solutions aligns perfectly with the spirit of resilience we champion.

We are especially grateful for your steadfast support of Resilient Recovery NC and our mission to rebuild communities devastated by Hurricane Helene. Your contributions—both in resources and advocacy—have been instrumental in helping us bring hope and strength back to those who lost everything. Thank you for standing with us in the fight for self-determination, freedom, and the promise of a better future. We are proud to call you a partner in resilience and liberty.

REFERENCES

Ames, B. N. (1979). Identifying environmental chemicals causing mutations and cancer. Science, 204(4393), 587-593.

Artman, J. (2024). Own Your Purpose: A Guide to Personal Accountability and Growth. Self-published.

Aurelius, M. (2002). Meditations (G. Long, Trans.). Penguin Classics. (Original work published c. 180 CE)

Aurelius, M. (2002). Meditations. Modern Library.

Beck, A. T. (1979). Cognitive therapy and the emotional disorders. Penguin Books.

Beck, J. S. (2011). Cognitive behavior therapy: Basics and beyond (2nd ed.). Guilford Press.

Bernstein, E. (2021). "Performing a cognitive reappraisal isn't turning off your negative thoughts." The Wall Street Journal. Retrieved from [WSJ Website]

Bezos, J. (2021). Invent and Wander: The Collected Writings of Jeff Bezos. Harvard Business Review Press.

Brown, B. (2010). The Gifts of Imperfection: Let Go of Who You Think You're Supposed to Be and Embrace Who You Are. Hazelden Publishing.

Byron, K. (2002). Loving What Is: Four Questions That Can Change Your Life. Harmony Books.

Damon, W., Menon, J., & Bronk, K. C. (2003). The development of purpose during adolescence. Applied Developmental Science, 7(3), 119-128.

Davidson, R. J., & McEwen, B. S. (2012). Social influences on neuroplasticity: Stress and interventions to promote well-being. Nature Neuroscience, 15(5), 689-695.

Duckworth, A. (2016). Grit: The Power of Passion and Perseverance. Scribner.

Duckworth, A. (2016). Grit: The power of passion and perseverance. Scribner.

Duhigg, C. (2012). The power of habit: Why we do what we do in life and business. Random House.

Dweck, C. S. (2006). Mindset: The new psychology of success. Random House.

Epictetus. (2008). Discourses and selected writings. Penguin Classics.

Ferriss, T. (2007). The 4-Hour Workweek: Escape 9-5, Live Anywhere, and Join the New Rich. Crown Publishing Group.

Goleman, D. (1995). Emotional Intelligence: Why It Can Matter More Than IQ. Bantam Books.

Gretchen, R. (2009). The Happiness Project: Or, Why I Spent a Year Trying to Sing in the Morning, Clean My Closets, Fight Right, Read Aristotle, and Generally Have More Fun. HarperCollins.

Hanson, R. (2013). Hardwiring Happiness: The New Brain Science of Contentment, Calm, and Confidence. Harmony Books.

Hill, N. (1937). Think and grow rich. The Ralston Society.

Holiday, R. (2014). The Obstacle Is the Way: The Timeless Art of Turning Trials into Triumph. Portfolio.

Holiday, R. (2016). The Daily Stoic: 366 Meditations on Wisdom, Perseverance, and the Art of Living. Portfolio.

John Templeton Foundation. (2018). The psychology of purpose. Retrieved from https://www.templeton.org/

Journal of Occupational Health Psychology. (2022). The impact of physical and mental health on entrepreneurial success.

Kabat-Zinn, J. (1990). Full Catastrophe Living: Using the Wisdom of Your Body and Mind to Face Stress, Pain, and Illness. Bantam Dell.

Kahneman, D. (2011). Thinking, fast and slow. Farrar, Straus and Giroux.

Katie, B. (2002). Loving What Is: Four Questions That Can Change Your Life. Harmony Books.

Lazarus, R. S., & Folkman, S. (1984). Stress, Appraisal, and Coping. Springer.

Lyubomirsky, S. (2007). The How of Happiness: A New Approach to Getting the Life You Want. Penguin Books.

Marcus Aurelius. (2002). Meditations. Modern Library.

McEwen, B. S., & Stellar, E. (1993). Stress and the individual: Mechanisms leading to disease. Archives of Internal Medicine, 153(18), 2093-2101.

McGraw Hill Education. (2024). Workplace wellbeing: Positive outcomes for employees and entrepreneurs achieved by not working outside work hours. Retrieved from https://www.mheducation.com/highered/blog/2024/06/workplace-wellbeing-positive-outcomes-for-employees-and-entrepreneurs-are-achieved-by-not-working-outside-work-hours.html

Morgan, T. H., Sturtevant, A. H., Muller, H. J., & Bridges, C. B. (1915). "The Mechanism of Mendelian Heredity." Henry Holt and Company.

Operating from scarcity induces fight, flight, or freeze responses, severely limiting problem-solving capabilities. Persistent focus on deficits fosters a perpetual sense of inadequacy, hindering future planning and decision-making. This scarcity mindset reinforces self-defeating actions, perpetuating negative cycles. Shifting toward abundance, as highlighted by Shafir (2013) in "Scarcity: Why Having Too Little Means So Much," frees mental bandwidth, enabling constructive problem-solving and clearer decision-making.

Resilience is the process of negotiating, managing and adapting to significant sources of stress or trauma. Assets and resources within the individual, their life and environment facilitate this capacity for adaptation and 'bouncing back' in the face of adversity. Across the life course, the experience of resilience will vary." — Usher K, et al. (2021)

Rotter, J. B. (1954). Social learning and clinical psychology. Prentice-Hall.

Rubin, G. (2009). The Happiness Project: Or, Why I Spent a Year Trying to Sing in the Morning, Clean My Closets, Fight Right, Read Aristotle, and Generally Have More Fun. HarperCollins.

Sapolsky, R. M. (2004). Why Zebras Don't Get Ulcers. Henry Holt and Company.

Selye, H. (1956). The Stress of Life. McGraw-Hill.

Seneca. (2015). Letters from a Stoic. Penguin Classics.

Shafir, E., & Mullainathan, S. (2013). Scarcity: Why Having Too Little Means So Much. Times Books.

Shapiro, F. (1989). Eye movement desensitization: A new treatment for post-traumatic stress disorder. Journal of Behavior Therapy and Experimental Psychiatry, 20(3), 211-217.

Shapiro, F. (2001). Eye movement desensitization and reprocessing: Basic principles, protocols, and procedures. Guilford Press.

Sinek, S. (2009). Start With Why: How Great Leaders Inspire Everyone to Take Action. Portfolio.

Skinner, B. F. (1953). Science and human behavior. Free Press.

Social Learning Theory, developed by psychologist Julian Rotter (1954) describes what he called the "Locus of Control" which refers to an individual's perception about the underlying main causes of events in his/her life. Said more simply, Do they believe that the events that unfold in their life are controlled by external forces (god, fate, luck, others), that they are just merely a product of circumstance or are they the ones in control. This can be broken down into two ends of a spectrum:

Usher, K., et al. (2021). Defining resilience: Negotiation, management, and adaptation to adversity. Retrieved from https://www.ncbi.nlm.nih.gov/

Vander Laan, R. (2009). Faith Lessons: That the World May Know. Zondervan.

Wallace, B. A. (2007). The Attention Revolution: Unlocking the Power of the Focused Mind. Wisdom Publications.

www.ingramcontent.com/pod-product-compliance
Lightning Source LLC
Chambersburg PA
CBHW071153070526
44584CB00019B/2771